T0056073

Islam and the West

Islam and the West

A Conversation with Jacques Derrida

MUSTAPHA CHÉRIF

Translated by
Teresa Lavender Fagan

With a foreword by
Giovanna Borradori

The University of Chicago Press ❋ Chicago and London

MUSTAPHA CHÉRIF is professor of philosophy and Islamic studies at the University of Algiers and a visiting professor at the Collège de France.

Among TERESA LAVENDER FAGAN's most recent translations are Rémi Brague's *The Wisdom of the World,* Jean Bottéro's *The Oldest Cuisine in the World,* and Alain Boureau's *Satan the Heretic: The Birth of Demonology in the Medieval West.*

Originally published as *L'Islam et l'occident. Rencontre avec Jacques Derrida* © Editions Odile Jacob, 2006.

The University of Chicago Press, Chicago 60637
The University of Chicago Press, Ltd., London
© 2008 by The University of Chicago
All rights reserved. Published 2008
Printed in the United States of America
17 16 15 14 13 12 11 10 09 08   1 2 3 4 5
ISBN-13: 978-0-226-10286-3 (cloth)
ISBN-10: 0-226-10286-6 (cloth)

Library of Congress Cataloging-in-Publication Data
Derrida, Jacques.
Islam and the West : a conversation with Jacques Derrida / Mustapha Chérif; translated by Teresa Lavender Fagan; with a foreword by Giovanna Borradori.
p. cm.
ISBN-13: 978-0-226-10286-3 (cloth : alk. paper)
ISBN-10: 0-226-10286-6 (pbk. : alk. paper)
1. Derrida, Jacques—Interviews. 2. East and West. 3. Political science—Philosophy. I. Chérif, Mustapha, 1950– II. Fagan, Teresa Lavender. III. Borradori, Giovanna. IV. Title.
CB251.D4 2008
909'.09767—dc22

                              2008003988

*To all those who unconditionally
welcome, listen to, and respect
THE OTHER.*

*With my thanks and gratitude to Madame Marguerite Derrida,
and to Professor Jean-Luc Nancy, who was kind
enough to read and comment on this work.*

Contents

Foreword:
Pure Faith in Peace

I want to speak here, today, as an Algerian, as an Algerian who became French at a given moment, lost his French citizenship, and then recovered it.

JACQUES DERRIDA

It is a late afternoon in the spring of 2003. In the tearoom of the Institut du Monde Arabe, in Paris, a man by the name of Mustapha Chérif is sitting at a table, deeply immersed in his thoughts. He is expecting the arrival of Jacques Derrida, thinker of worldwide fame, controversial philosopher, and prophet of the oppressed, the undocumented, and the unseen.

We can imagine what Chérif could have reasonably anticipated: after greeting Derrida and exchanging a few words of gratitude for agreeing to participate in the ensuing public debate, they would have walked toward the hall where a large audience would be eagerly awaiting them. But Chérif could not have anticipated that Derrida would be coming straight from the hospital, where he had just learned he was suffering from pancreatic cancer, the illness that would kill him fifteen months later. "For any other meeting I wouldn't have had the strength to participate," Derrida told Chérif, who found his participation "the most beautiful sign of solidarity, the greatest gesture of friendship he could have offered" (p. 97).

This slender book is the earnest transcript of what Chérif and Derrida told each other that late afternoon, with Derrida's ominous diagnosis in the background. Focusing on the crucial but largely underestimated role that Algeria, his country of birth, has played in Derrida's philosophical itinerary, *Islam and the West* presents Derrida's interpretation of the interdependence of politics, religion, and faith in a new light; shows that his ideal of "democracy to come" has a strong universalist component; and, finally, adds to his fascinating understanding not only of Islam but of the Arab as the ultimate figure of exclusion and dissidence in the post-9/11 era.

Admittedly, Chérif and Derrida are an odd couple, for their profound love of Algeria is almost all they share. A vocal public intellectual and one of the only moderate Islamic voices speaking up today, Chérif has consistently worked from within the institutions he hopes to affect. Once a prominent politician, serving in the Algerian government as secretary of higher education and ambassador to Egypt, this professor of epistemology and Islamic studies at the University of Algiers was the first Muslim thinker to be received by a pope in the Vatican's history. In November 2006, after giving a controversial speech on the violent nature of Islam in Ratisbon, Germany, and just before his politically delicate visit to Turkey, Benedict XVI invited Chérif into his private library for a tête à tête, without witnesses, on the dialogue of civilizations.

By contrast, Derrida never fit any institutional cadre. Throughout his life and in many different forms, Derrida aimed at unearthing and dismantling, or deconstructing, the oppressive force that he saw inhabiting all institutions, simply because of their regulating and normalizing role. Understanding institutions in this fashion allowed Derrida to broaden the traditional notion of what counts as an institution. Traditionally, institutions are understood to shape the concrete domains of education, law, politics, and religion. For Derrida, abstract conceptual constructs such as gender, ethnicity, and language govern human existence in a similar way and thus may be counted as institutions. Deconstruction, as the process of identification and displacement of the oppressive structure proper to all institutions, can be indiscriminately applied to either the concrete or the conceptual domain. In Derrida's reading, even nonreligious institutions tend to impose their norms and standards from the top down, according to a model of absolute authority shared by the three religions of the Book: Judaism, Christianity, and Islam. If this is true, which Derrida believes it is, the liberating duty of deconstruction entails a commitment to secularization (*laïcité*), assumed as the interminable effort to dismantle the theocratic model of institutional authority, which coincides with the demand for unconditional submission.

In light of Derrida's suspicion of all institutional formats, it is not surprising that he requested an informal conversation with Chérif. And it is to Chérif's credit to have produced a book in line with Derrida's original desire: a narrative that progresses without a predetermined path and that is presented to the reader as a "stream of consciousness." And yet, for all his preference for fluidity over rigidity, Derrida was a highly guarded man, whose constant effort to protect his private life was obvious even to those of us who knew him personally over a span of many years.

This book pierces that reticence at a moment of great vulnerability, revealing the depth and complexity of Derrida's feelings for Algeria. Chérif knows it and, in the appendix entitled "Biography: Derrida and the Southern Shores," gives the reader the bare facts that lie behind those feelings. Some of these are well known and some less. Among those rarely discussed is that, after leaving Algeria for the first time in 1949 at the age of nineteen, Derrida returned as a soldier in the French Army and a teacher in 1957–59, during Algeria's war of independence. Chérif notes Derrida's first and only return to lecture at the University of Algiers in 1971. Interestingly, over the course of the next two decades Derrida would travel all over Africa and the Middle East, expressing his political support for the oppressed in South Africa and in the Occupied Palestinian Territories, for example. But he would never again land in his country of birth. When, in 1991, a second trip to Algeria was planned, the visit was abruptly canceled because of the Gulf War. The very last opportunity would have been in November 2004, when he had been invited to a conference entirely dedicated to his work. But, as Chérif sadly acknowledges, destiny decided otherwise, for Derrida died on October 8 of that year.

The book leaves us to ponder the eerie coincidence of Derrida expressing his deepest feelings about Algeria just prior to his death. Chérif would like the reader to believe that even the master of deconstruction had a dream: an Algeria in which French and Algerians could live together in harmony. But here is where, I believe, the difference in their sensibilities emerges most clearly. Long before his conversation with Chérif, Derrida chose to name his affection for Algeria "nostalgeria" (*nostalgérie*), a designation expressing his characteristic blend of theoretical sophistication and emotional control. Nostalgeria captures the fact that Derrida's love of, and hope for, Algeria was never that of a citizen, involving the patriotic attachment one has for a nation-state. In a speech in support of Algerian intellectuals, delivered in 1994 while the country was experiencing unspeakable violence, Derrida claimed that the attachment of the noncitizen is all the more powerful because it can afford to tie, in a single knot, the heart, the mind, and the act of taking a political stance. Heart, mind, and the act of taking a political stance form the cardinal points of nostalgeria, which is a constellation more than an entity: it is an irreducible plurality of different emotional and rational strains, protected from all oppression, including the oppression of the modern institution par excellence, the nation-state.

The way in which Algeria colored both the birth and the death of this great thinker is swiftly but delicately painted by Chérif's farewell to Derrida. Entitled "From the Southern Shores, Adieu to Derrida," this afterword was the eulogy Chérif read at the Collège International de Philosophie, in Paris, on October 21, 2004. In 1983, Derrida and a small group of friends conceived and founded this "anti-institution," where a new practice of thinking and exchanging philosophy was intended to take place. In 2003, at the commemoration of its twentieth anniversary, Derrida underlined the noninstitutional character of this institution by declaring that the birth of the Collège had not been the result of a comprehensive plan but rather the culmination of a series of setbacks.

Among the many quirky aspects of this book, the most evident is perhaps its title. The project of reconciling Islam and the West presupposes that there is only one Islam and one West. By contrast, and this is perhaps the key argument of the book, there is plurality *in* Islam as well as multiple Islams, as there is plurality *in* the West as well as multiple Wests. This consideration supports Chérif and Derrida's invitation to rethink the Islam-West opposition in terms of the internal division of the Mediterranean Sea into Southern and Northern shores. "Derrida came from the Southern shores," Chérif writes, thus "he viewed Islam and Muslim culture without external prejudice" (p. 7). Concurrently, Derrida admits to being very sensitive to the opportunity of feeling welcome "among Algerians," to which he adds, "I cherish that which is still Algerian in me, what is in me and keeps me Algerian" (p. 86).

The use of either set of categories, Islam and the West and the Northern and Southern shores of the Mediterranean, identifies two separate ways of addressing a politically sensitive issue. In the United States, in most social sciences including Islamic studies, political theory, and philosophy, to see legitimacy in the opposition Islam-West means to align oneself with the "culturalists," represented by conservative scholars like Bernard Lewis and Samuel Huntington. For both of them, Islam is about the blending of the distinction between politics and religion. This is the keystone of their culturalist explanation of current tensions in terms of the clash of civilizations. By contrast, progressive Islamic scholars in Europe and the United States, including Olivier Roy and Mahmoud Mamdani, oppose that categorization, preferring instead the Northern versus Southern distinction. Conceiving of Islam and the West as the Southern and Northern shores of the Mediterranean basin means to interpret them as the two halves of a geographical, ethnic, religious, and cultural unit. It also gestures at a concept of religious and cultural identity that is intrinsically and irreducibly divided. There are at least two internal divisions that unite the Mediterranean basin, giving it its unique identity. One is the division and overlapping of the three major monotheistic traditions that originated from it: Christianity, Judaism, and Islam. The other, more painful one, is the unforgivable attack that European colonialism launched against the Muslim world. The Mediterranean is a unity only with reference to both of these constitutive divisions.

Chérif and Derrida align themselves with the progressive antiorientalist lineage in hopes, as Chérif wrote, to "to reopen the horizon, to go beyond the divisions, to seek a new form of alliance between individuals and peoples in love with justice" (p. 11). But who is passionate about justice? Is it the Northern self or the Southern other? Or is it, rather, the reverse: the Southern self and the Northern other? Is the Muslim a figure of what is near (*du proche*) or of what is far away (*du lointain*)? And who is Derrida's neighbor: this proximity or this distance?

With his first question, Chérif opens a window onto Derrida's "lived experience as an Algerian" (*vécu d'Algérien*) or, more precisely, as a French-Maghrebin-Jew, or maybe simply as an Arab-Jew, a condition of marginalization similar to the one that a large portion of Arab youth is living in France today. The essence of Derrida's answer is that to be such a hybrid meant for him to form a conception of the other as the closest of all possible neighbors (*l'autre comme le prochain le plus proche*). To be at home is, thus, to feel the absolute otherness of one's neighbor. In this way, *Islam and the West* reinforces one of Derrida's key persuasions: that civilization and community are not about sameness but difference. The Greek, the Arab, and the Jew, the three figures at the center of the second half of this book, define Mediterranean civilization precisely because of their irreducible difference.

To dissolve the opposition between Islam and the West within the divided unity of Mediterranean civilization is one of the leading themes of the discussion between Chérif and Derrida. Both of them register the force of this new categorization, which expands upon a major shift in vocabulary that occurred after World War II.

Pure Faith in Peace

As intellectuals, historians, and philosophers tried to make sense of the tragedy of the Holocaust in the context of the Western ideals of equality and freedom, democracy, and fraternity, they faced the moral obligation to call into question the unity of the West as a fundamentally Christian concept. The redefinition of the Western trunk in Judeo-Christian terms emerged in this context.

Notwithstanding the massive difference in scale, the terrorist attacks of 9/11 and the international mayhem of their aftermath, have increased the need to pluralize the Western trunk even further. "Universal civilization belongs to everyone and is owned by no one," Chérif said, indicating that "the *Greek, Arab,* and *Jewish* peoples represented three major historical moments in the civilization of the Mediterranean basin" (p. 37). Derrida's parallel call "to deconstruct the European intellectual construct of Islam" (p. 38) adds a personal dimension to the historical and ethical scopes of Chérif's position:

> The community to which I belonged was cut off in three ways: it was cut off first both from the Arab and the Berber, actually the Maghrebin language and culture; it was also cut off from the French, indeed European, language and culture, which were viewed as distant poles, unrelated to its history; and finally, or to begin with, it was cut off from the Jewish memory, from that history and that language that one must assume to be one's own, but which at a given moment no

longer were—at least in a special way, for most of its members in a sufficiently living and internal way. The arrogant specificity, the traumatizing brutality of what is called the colonial war, colonial cruelty—some, including myself, experienced it from both sides, if I may say so. (pp. 34–35)

The vaccine against the colonial brutality that all Algerians know firsthand is for Chérif the universalism of democracy. But Derrida cautions him that the universalism of democracy presupposes that democracy not be conceived as a fixed model of a political regime. "What distinguishes the idea of democracy from all other ideas of political regimes—monarchy, aristocracy, oligarchy, and so on—is that democracy is the only political system, a model without a model, that accepts its own historicity, that is, its own future, which accepts its self-criticism, which accepts its perfectibility" (p. 42). This concept of democracy, which is undeniably Greek in origin, inherits from its beginnings an association with the land, a conception of the "right to belong" based on being born in a territory, which coincides with the boundaries of the state. "I have nothing against the State, I have nothing against citizenship, but I dare to dream of a democracy that is not simply tied to a nation-state and to citizenship. And it is under these conditions that one can speak of a universal democracy, a democracy that is not only cosmopolitical but universal" (pp. 43–44). The universalism of democracy consists precisely in its being the model for the absence of a model, that is, of a universally applicable system of governance. This is why it cannot be packaged and exported as one pleases.

Chérif's view of Islam may be the last bastion of resistance against the complete commodification of existence pushed South by the Northern winds of extreme secularism and antireligious sentiment. "Can Islam," he asks, "that object of misunderstanding, a figure of the resistant, the dissident, the other, contribute to loosening the deadlock?" (p. 14). If it can, it is because Islam's core is the question of the meaning of human existence, or what Chérif calls a relation to mystery (*le rapport au mystère*). Is faith the translation of that mystery, which is the mystery of the elusiveness of the meaning of existence in the face of the divine?

For Derrida, faith is indeed the Judeo-Christian correlative of mystery except that there is nothing mysterious about faith. "I cannot address the other, whoever he or she might be, regardless of his or her religion, language, culture, without asking that other to believe me and to trust me [*me faire crédit*]. One's relationship to the other, addressing the other, presupposes faith" (pp. 57–58). Faith is thus the condition of my relation with the other in a social context. It is the social bond itself, which would not exist without the ability to have faith in another human being. And yet, for Derrida religion and faith are two separate domains. Intolerance and the conflict with secularized politics and culture pertains to religion, because religion is by definition exclusionary: there are many religions, and most of them are mutually exclusive. But since the relation to the other presupposes faith, there is no contradiction at all between the secularization of politics and what Chérif calls "the mystery of life."

For Chérif, Derrida is the model for how one should think of one's roots: from the perspective of the question concerning the meaning of existence. The question concerning the meaning of existence is the Universal. Islam, and the figure of the Arab that impersonates it, is the last dissident opposing the downturns of global modernity. Therefore, both Islam and the Arab have taken up the role of universal target. Islam is a religion and not a culture—this is Chérif's firm belief, which he offers here on behalf of the silent majority of moderate Muslims who condemn the manipulation of religion for political violence.

The lack of teaching of true religion and an indoctrination based on a retrograde vision of the spiritual have produced misguided or fanatic individuals. Whereas the Classical West was Judeo-Islamo-Christian and Greco-Arab, we have been led to believe that it was only Greco-Roman and Judeo-Christian. The sons

of Abraham fall into the trap of confrontation at the
moment when they must live together. On the European side, Islamic studies are envisioned from the perspective of security: this reductive view favors integration and denigration and reduces the third branch of
monotheism to a myriad of small groups. As for the
Muslims, one must deplore the weakness of their objective thinking and critical theology. (p. 3)

Derrida's way to cut the Gordian knot of fanaticism and the ideological manipulation of religion
for political purposes is, unsurprisingly, by focusing
on pure faith. The issue of faith is, for him, essential
to the peace process. To Chérif's question regarding how intellectuals can oppose the forces of closure and separatism, Derrida answered, "One cannot
force someone to speak or to listen; this is where the
question of faith returns. An opening up must occur where there is war, and there is war everywhere
in the world today. Peace is only possible when one
of the warring sides takes the first step, the hazardous initiative, the risk of opening up dialogue, and
decides to make the gesture that will lead not only
to an armistice but to peace" (p. 59). To take the initiative, full of promise as well as risk, is to embrace
faith. Peace is thus in the hands of an act of faith in
the other, both on the Northern and on the Southern
shores of the Mediterranean.

GIOVANNA BORRADORI

Foreword

Introduction:
Friendship, Above All

I wish to share here my encounter and my conversation with a major philosopher of our time, for this is the duty of friendship. I am convinced that friendship, respect for the other, listening to the other, are proof that one grasps that which demands understanding. I want this "sharing," if you will, to be a testimony that debate, discussion, dialogue are more essential than ever. Current events are irrevocable: the West and the East are living in a state of intolerance or, at the very least, in an absence of dialogue and in misunderstanding. How did we arrive at the ignorance, tension, and hatred so shamelessly flaunted by some? At this precise moment, for example, when we so greatly need to engage in dialogue, the climate of the times seems turned toward xenophobia, on the one

hand, and toward fanaticism, on the other. Beyond
the aftermaths of the past, whose influence we know
so well, after the end of the cold war, the propaganda
of the "clash of civilizations" and the hegemonic am-
bitions of the primary world power create a situation
of uncertainty, disorder, and hatred toward Islam.
This downward spiraling has taken us to the occupa-
tion of Iraq, the intensification of the suffering of the
Palestinian people, and to an impasse in any attempt
at a partnership between the two shores of the Mediterranean. The retreat of the law and the policy of
"double standards" have exacerbated the resentment
of Muslims, who are considered the "new enemies"
in an aim to divert attention away from the political
problems of the world. Other peoples, even the Israeli
people, have nothing to gain from this.

The movements that usurp the name of Islam and
exploit religion in the political realm are intoxicated
by this situation of injustice. Traumatizing terrorist reactions, the actions of the desperate Palestinians who
are pushed to commit suicide by brutal repression and
lack of hope, the infamous seizing of hostages—but
also the restrictive practices of religion—all of this is
harmful to Muslims. Injustices, on the one hand, and
irrational reactions, on the other, have thus brought
to the forefront a global tragedy of hatred.

In this context of the terrorism of the powerful and
the terrorism of the weak, efforts toward peace appear hopeless. Those who promote hatred, who are

nonetheless in the minority, have won a battle, but they have not yet destroyed the future. Today, the extremists in every camp have more influence than men and women of peace. If we remain silent, the situation will only get worse. The media give most of their attention to the violence-mongers, and some intellectuals, or those who claim the title, despise the other, reject the right to be different, and claim to hold the truth in the name of scientific rationality and scientism!

Ignorance is the primary cause of hatred. In the North and in the South, education has abandoned a common base; and we have seen a decrease in the study of the culture of the other. The lack of teaching of true religion and an indoctrination based on a retrograde vision of the spiritual have produced misguided or fanatic individuals. Whereas the Classical West was Judeo-Islamo-Christian and Greco-Arab, we have been led to believe that it was only Greco-Roman and Judeo-Christian. The sons of Abraham fall into the trap of confrontation at the moment when they must live together. On the European side, Islamic studies are envisioned from the perspective of security: this reductive view favors integration and denigration and reduces the third branch of monotheism to a myriad of small groups. As for the Muslims, one must deplore the weakness of their objective thinking and critical theology. One hears above all only the apologetic discourse of preachers who lapse into sectarian politics or that of intellectuals of dilution, self-proclaimed "new reformers" who, from outside the faith, propose the application of recipes of positivism to the Koran.

Fortunately, the majority of Muslims live their faith peacefully; they refuse the howling of the wolves who call for intolerance, as well as the siren song that calls for depersonalization. We are all, believers and nonbelievers, caught up in the same movement of the world. Our ancestors didn't see the coming of the time of colonization, close to two centuries ago, nor of fascism, more than sixty years ago. Our duty today is to attempt to foresee that which threatens to occur in these times stricken with harshness and incomprehension.

Beyond their current weaknesses and their backwardness in matters of democracy, Muslims are attempting to resist in two ways: against that which is urgent—that is, against injustice—and also, on a fundamental level, against that which appears to be a *de-signification* of the world, a challenging of the very foundations of humanity as it has existed since the time of Abraham. To some, such resistance is an intolerable dissidence. Those people stigmatize the eternal "Saracen" who becomes a target of hatred because of his resistance to the decadence of modernity and his opposition to justice. But such resistance doesn't involve either nostalgia for tradition or defense of religion. It is the meaning of humanity itself that is at issue. How can one confront the end of a world, even if it is not the end of the world? The separation of religion and politics is, on this point, a vital truism: contrary to what is believed, Islam does not confuse these two realms. But a hatred of the spiritual—felt by some—and the fear of a freedom suspected of being only license and permissiveness—which obsesses others—accelerates dehumanization. The return of the religious, whether in the legitimate form of a search for spiritual experience or in the illegitimate form of fundamentalist practices, is the reflection of a break between morality and life, between responsibility and freedom.

On the political level, in spite of the prodigious progress of science, in spite of advances in matters relating to human rights, many people realize that the commercialization of the world reduces their capacity to be responsible and to freely decide their future. Indeed, the ability to think, to think in other terms, is challenged by the shrinking of a horizon diminished by an absence of meaning, a breaking of ties, and a dictatorship of the market—and this is all aggravated by the phenomenon of terrorism. The tendency is to impose a reductive version of the human. In order to create a diversion, we are led to believe that belief in general, and Islam in particular, is only obscurantism, representing the worst of alienations, and that only scientism and atheism have emancipatory force. As a reaction, some believers shut themselves off in a thoughtless way and espouse an intolerant practice of religion. But hatred, every kind of hatred, is doomed to failure. Without an ally, without dialogue, and without sound thinking, we cannot loosen the stranglehold in which people are gripped. For these things I now call upon a master, a philosopher whom we miss so very much, in whose presence some would not have dared to speak as they speak today, with so much casualness and hatred toward the different other and in the face of the questions that confront us. This thinker is our friend Jacques Derrida. In this book I will tell how I came to interview him and to talk with him one late afternoon in the spring of 2003.

I had attempted to prepare my questions and to give them to Derrida before the day of our meeting. His busy schedule and his frail health prevented me from doing so. The day of the meeting his openness and kindness made my work easy. We met and spoke first, just the two of us, in the tearoom of the Institut du Monde Arabe. We were going to speak in front of a large audience. I hoped to demonstrate clarity, caution, humility; and I wanted to discuss his approach as a "nonreligious" thinker who, as a philosopher and from outside a system of belief, attempted to deal with problematics of religion. For me, he was a thinker who did not despise religion and who had introduced a new form of discourse: he reclaimed for religion questions dealing with the realm of the spiritual, thus interrogating religion in a nonreligious, purely rational way. In so doing, Derrida asked a new question, inaugurating an approach that modern philosophy adopts in an obscure and perplexing way. As a Muslim intellectual, while I sought enlightenment and guidance from him, for my part, I wished to explain the specificity of Islam, that object of misunderstanding. Furthermore, since Derrida came from the Southern shores, he viewed Islam and Muslim culture without external prejudice. I began to read his work more than thirty years ago. I read him passionately, patiently, and with surprise too. For me, it was difficult reading. As I was taught by the *falsafa* thinkers, and even by the mystical tradition on another level, Derrida taught me that meaning can only be shared, that meaning goes beyond individuals, beyond all factions, that there is a separate meaning, that its value is worthy in and of itself, independent of interventions, appropriations, demands. There is a noble moral dimension in Derrida's thinking: he is concerned with the future of human dignity. His is a philosophical thinking that practices the critical spirit to an incredible degree. It is located a thousand miles from the vain attempts to restore meaning, from all the *returns to*, and one hundred steps from any habituation to disorientation, to the absence of meaning. Derrida forces us to really think so we will be prepared to face the dilemmas of an era in which the question of meaning represents the essential problem.

Friendship, Above All

What better way to be open to that meaning than by conversing with the different and dissimilar other, who is par excellence the Muslim, figure of the close and the distant? In the four corners of the world, Europeanization, Westernization, Americanization, with all their failures and their advances, engender convulsions, silent revolts, illusions, disappointments, alienating forms of repulsion/attraction, with everything aggravated by the globalization of fractures and inequalities. Resistance and dissidence, whether they come from good sense or from irrational movements, are quite real even in the Muslim world, whose foundations have begun to be shaken, since no one, even under the threat of death, can stop *progress.*

It is not enough to question the meaning of existence, to compare values, texts, practices: the dichotomy between East and West is intensified in the global context. Nor is it enough to band together against the *irrational.* We must try to grasp the ineffable, to understand why and how reason, on the one hand, and faith, on the other, experience such difficulties in describing metamorphoses, in facing them, in accepting them. It is true that faith, as an intuition, sensation, conviction, lives and grasps the signs, risks, movements of the world in an easy, simple, and natural way; from that, when it gives itself the Open for a horizon, it enables the human being to maintain a stand, a dignity, an ethics, even if nothing guarantees happiness. But reason, too, when it refrains from excesses and from claiming to govern meaning completely, when the unconditional is its principle and the infinite its task, can and must promote worthy, moral, and humane behavior. Together, beings from the East and the West, thirsty for reason and for justice, meaning, openness—together, not separately—let us talk, discuss, analyze in order to endure the trial imposed on all humans: let us not substitute anything for this Open that is both absent and unspeakably present. Obviously, the questions I asked the philosopher did not directly confront the formidable theme of the relation between reason and faith: our discussion bore more generally on the political problems of the world today and on the future of civilizations. All the same, the theme of the relationship between reason and faith constantly remained as an undercurrent in our conversation.

This discussion took place in friendship, consent, respect, listening. I, the Algerian intellectual that I am, attempted to question Derrida, a great master of modern philosophy and a native of Algeria. Our conversation centered around the open questions of our time: the universal, secularization, our relation to the other, the connections between worlds, between Islam and the West, the dialogue of civilizations, the link between logic and meaning when the horizon seems no longer to contain them, freedom, justice, democracy at a time when the law of the jungle prevails. None of these themes was dealt with lightly,

Friendship, Above All

9

are overcome by techno-science, a crisis of values, and the world market. "Always choose life and endlessly assert survival," Derrida said with conviction at the end of his life. In my opinion, this statement establishes that from now on the goal of thinking is to help us get out of the impasses of despair and defeatism, and even more, to go beyond the traps and the false dilemmas of globalization that function as diversions from the true problems. We owe this inspiration to Derrida's audacity and openness as well as to his power of demonstration.

In this sense, we must understand what humanity and the human stand for, and what existence truly is, by, on the one hand, going beyond the corrupted forms of classical humanism and confronting them—for that humanism is caught in the web of waning Eurocentrism and of "the civilization of the death of God"—and, on the other hand, by rejecting the closed versions of religious traditionalisms in the grip of all sorts of upheavals, versions marked by the obscure return of the religious and the multiform madness of fundamentalism, intolerance, and terrorism. The strength of Derrida's responses, his elevated sense of an opening up, is the sign that assuming the task that has fallen upon us is still possible. This sign helps us not only to rethink concepts but also to participate in the formation of a common conscience, to go beyond all borders and to state a universal in which the specific, the different, the plural dimension forms the very foundation of the civilization to come, without ceding anything to the excesses of particularism. The secularization of the political and of the public spheres, Derrida rightly tells us, is the fundamental condition, the necessary passage to freedom, democracy, and progress. For the field that I know relatively well, Islamology, I will say with modesty that, without a shadow of a doubt, the principle of *secularity* is, despite appearances, intrinsic to Islam, and this has been true since its origins. And yet, the uniqueness of the third monotheistic religion resides in the fact that the different dimensions of life—religion and politics, the spiritual and the temporal, nature and culture, the public and the private—if they must naturally be separated in order to avoid confusion and to prevent all totalitarianisms, must not be placed in opposition. Their extreme separation can create a void, which reason cannot be counted on to fill.

In my opinion, it is clear that our modern era neutralizes or even eliminates politics as well as religion, that is, the two fundamental aspects of life. These two realms should neither be confused nor isolated, marginalized, cut off from life. How then, can a rational and rigorous thinker, who is also an authentic believer, reconsider the question of secularization, its meaning and its object, other than by simply separating the one from the other and by eliminating, as legitimately as possible, the claims of the theocratic power to govern? A task made even harder by the

Friendship, Above All

fact that, as objective modern thought stresses, most Western philosophical concepts are still imbued with their theological source and that reason continues to be fed, without admitting it, on predicates and references issued from Christianity, in spite of the *designification* of the world and the ravaging effects of a dominant, largely anticlerical, nonreligious, and atheist ideology. On the one hand, the greeting addressed to the other, the unconditional acceptance of the other beyond all differences, and, on the other, the infinite exercise of reason, are, Derrida tells us, among the ways that lead to secularization, to the democracy to come. From our perspective, as Muslims, the task of thought is to interrogate the new condition of humanity, which is today confronted with a foundationless world in which religion abandons life, in which both the ability for the individual to be a free person and the possibility for a people to assume its responsibilities are challenged. In this context, I believe that Islam is blamed for everything: both for being apolitical—that is, incapable of a project of the City that founds freedom and equality—and for being excessively political and confusing various political and religious levels, with modernity presenting itself as an apolitical and transparent space—which is far from corresponding to reality.

Can Islam, that object of misunderstanding, a figure of the resistant, the dissident, the other, contribute to loosening the deadlock? Can Islam help to rediscover not so much the forms of the religious that accept either doubtful compromises or fundamentalist retraction but a reasonable reason and a vital faith, both capable of opening the horizon of the world without turning away either from the urgencies and challenges of the earth—the temporal—or from the demands of that which is beyond the world—the spiritual? If this were not to occur, the politico-religious extremists, on the one hand, and the antireligious extremists, on the other, in flagrant contradiction with their respective founding values—Revelation and Faith, for the former, Greek thought and Enlightenment philosophy for the latter—would only aggravate the already very critical situation of the world by advancing either dogma and imprisonment in blind reaction or the commercialization of the temple and of life. Those who participate in the conspiracy against the spiritual in general and Islam in particular, which is also a conspiracy against the freedom of mankind, misunderstand and deform the perspectives of religion, notably of Islam. They miss both the opportunity to question the problems and the issues that underlie our humanity and the possibility to be prepared for the transformations necessary to discern the future. And they lack the ability to understand how the ultimate monotheistic religion can participate in a reflection on the future, beyond all differences and without succumbing to a return to the myths of the ones and the others. The obsessive animosity of some in the

North regarding the spiritual, monotheism, and Islam in particular and the animosity of others in the South concerning secularity and autonomy reveal the abysmal current global crisis.

Like Maurice Blanchot, Jean-Toussaint Desanti, Gilles Deleuze, Gérard Granel, Jean-Luc Nancy, and other philosophers at the forefront of modern thought, Derrida's approach shows that it is not too late to attempt to unconditionally open up both modern reason and religious faith, together and separately, each in its own realm, to the greatest possible demands, beyond the limits and the risks, the diversions, and the responsibilities of our time. The closing of the horizon, the negative trends and difficulties in reason and religion, the new historical monstrosities assailing us are perhaps not definitive, insurmountable, nor invincible, if we at least understand that we mustn't either idolize reason as opposed to faith, or vice versa, or simply tolerate one while preferring the other. Rather, our mission should be to open them up, raise them, carry them along, each in its own unique domain, lift them up to the heights of that which is worth living for: the free search for the beautiful, the just, and the true. The questions I asked Jacques Derrida, the opinions I expressed,[1] did not broach these more than arduous themes head-on. I formulated them, so

---

1 I transcribed the text of our conversation myself. Jacques Derrida wasn't able to read it or even listen to it again.

to speak, like confidences: an Algerian intellectual, involved in the act of thinking, who is worried about the disorder in the world will tell how he spoke with a great European philosopher, forever the friend of the other. *Friendship above all*—this is my horizon.

The Future of Civilizations

My conversation with Jacques Derrida, as I am relating it in this book, took place during the final gathering of the Algerian-French colloquium I led on the theme "The Future of Civilizations." As a tribute to the eminent figures in the dialogue among civilizations during the twentieth century, the goal of the event was to question the great philosopher on the difficulties of our time, to hear him sketch, in front of a large audience, a few elements of his answers to the essential questions of our somber era. A related objective was to remind everyone of the necessity of turning toward a common future, made of sharing and mutual knowledge, rather than inequality and incomprehension.

Why was the colloquium held? The disturbing world context more than ever forces people of good will to communicate in order to reject the theory of the "clash of civilizations"; even more important, we must attempt to discover a new horizon for living together. Three goals were set forth: first, to keep alive the common memory among peoples; second, to carry out a severe criticism, a "deconstruction," of our downfalls; and third, to clarify what should be done for the future.

The colloquium "Algeria-France: Tribute to the Great Figures of the Dialogue between Civilizations" that was held at the Institut du Monde Arabe in Paris, May 26 and 27, 2003, was a perfect opportunity to attempt to clarify the problematics of dialogue and to help people everywhere turn toward a future of sharing and of mutual understanding. Orientalism, despite its contradictions, its limitations, and its connections with colonization in the nineteenth and twentieth centuries, has nevertheless enabled a certain knowledge of, approach to, and curiosity about the Orient, in particular about the cultures and societies of the Southern shores of the Mediterranean. Today, following the fall of the Berlin Wall in 1989, and even more after September 11, 2001, everyone senses there is a serious threat, primarily due to a retreat from knowledge and a misunderstanding of the other: the thoughtless, arbitrary, and unjust designation of a "new enemy," that is, Islam. Furthermore, reciprocal ignorance foreshadows the risks of a supposed "clash of cultures." Within certain decision-making circles in the West, centralism and power in all their forms produce policies that harm peace, the good working of international relations, and a balance between nations. In addition, modernity, under the pretext that it is presented in the form of external aggression, is rejected by small, but vocal, groups in the South.

And yet there is no inevitable confrontation nor intrinsic clash of civilizations in the history of the relations between the two worlds. On the contrary, Islam has participated in the emergence of the modern Western world; through its cultural and spiritual values, it is close to Judeo-Christian and Greco-Roman ethics, norms, and principles, regardless of the very real differences, divergences. and uniqueness of each. Today, humanity is confronted with multiple challenges; will the generations to come be the complete authors of the life they will lead, and will they be able to live on the basis of their own ability to assume a multicultural existence? Within the framework of the very negative globalization in its current forms, the shrinking of rights and the difficulty of being a responsible citizen, will the quest for happiness and freedom, dignity and humanity in life still be possible tomorrow?

No culture, or religion, can face these challenges and respond fully alone, for in the face of the complexity of the situation it is the universal that leads.

The Future of Civilizations

The need for dialogue becomes all the more obvious since in the North as well as the South the vast majority of human beings prefer peace to war, exchange to ostracism, mutual respect to arrogance and exclusion.

It is not just a matter of simple dialogue; we must rediscover a common memory and heal the various forms of amnesia that feed hatred. Beyond the pains of the wars of colonization and their aftermaths, Islam and the West, Algeria and France, share common values. There are entire aspects of the culture of the Southern shores that have never been understood, integrated, or accepted by Western culture. In addition to revealing the common patrimony that has been hidden, it is everyone's duty to think about and reconsider the connections between the worlds and their cultures. To achieve a true dialogue, the common intellectual universe, the cultural horizon, and all historical references deserve new readings; they need to be reconsidered and criticized, in a new way. The hypothesis is not insignificant at a time when the new and unjust world order as well as the retrograde fundamentalist ideology, each in their own way, completely hide and demonize the other. To rethink globality, the future of the Mediterranean region, the West, and Islam, means leaving one's deep-seated beliefs and prejudices, sources of exclusion for some and of defense for others. We must return to more self-control, objectivity, wisdom, for it is a matter of the future of our being together, of humanity in its unity as well as its plurality.

The seriousness of the situation requires responding with reason and measure to questions such as, What should I do with the time I have to live with others? Coming together, in these somber times, is the beginning of a response and means that one cannot postpone asking the question. For Muslims it is urgent and imperative to undertake a deep and constructive self-criticism; a work of *ijtihad*, interpretation, and of *tajdid*, renewal, which should recall that the Koran and the words (*hadiths*) of the Prophet prescribe an opening up, democracy, and the universal. For the West, assuming there clearly exists a mastered problematic of the question of the political City, of the modern being, and of responsibility, which is not obvious, it must rethink the theme of its relationship with the other, in particular with the Muslim. Dialogue with the third monotheism that resists, even badly, is a major issue, especially since modern life itself seems increasingly built on the foundation of an exclusion of monotheism from the realm of the possible, on the rejection of religion, on the generalization of atheism, or of a reductive, false theism.

Within this framework, the logic of war and the globalization of injustice contradict the evoked principles of the rights of peoples and of human rights, the right to be different as well as access to an authentic universality. This forces us to rethink the present world, where everything appears unequal, unilateral, and exclusive, without a universal foundation, without ethics and without true representation of a balanced universe and humanity. To rethink this disturbing world, in which the right to be different is less and less a given, is a necessity that cannot be ignored.

Paying tribute to emblematic figures of the dialogue of civilizations, both Algerian and French, is part of this will to rethink the heritage, the concepts, and our evolving reality. This also means that encounters, exchange, synthesis are still possible. Algerian thinkers and men of faith from the past, from Mohamed Bencheneb (literary figure, 1869–1929) to Abdelhamid Ben Badis (father of Algerian reformism, 1889–1940), from Malek Bennabi (Islamologist, 1905–73) to Mehdi Bouabdelli (theologian and historian, 1907–92), and from France, from Louis Massignon (Orientalist and Islamologist, 1883–1962) to Jacques Berque (Orientalist and Islamologist, 1910–95), from Étienne-Léon Duval (Archbishop of Algiers, 1904–96) to Germaine Tillion (ethnologist, born in 1907), have all labored, each in his or her own way—and others today are continuing—in the quest for self through an encounter with the other. Those historical figures have pursued rapprochement and convergence, aware that joy in life is achieved by and through a just, vigilant, and fecund relationship with a different other. It is a matter of recognizing the dissimilarity, the ruptures, and the interruptions, everything that can and must concern us. The tribute to the great figures of the dialogue of civilizations aimed to note, at the highest level of thought, the discoveries of Algeria and France. Through dialogue there is an opportunity to express a gratitude, an attachment, and a faithfulness to the common memory of the two shores; to commit oneself to new perspectives on the relationships jeopardized by the diversions, the injustice, and the misunderstandings, diversions that are both those of modernity marked by the logic of war and those of the Muslim world in the form of violent Islamism. It is a matter of rejecting, through logical analysis among other things, the law of the strongest, blind violence, and all forms of exclusion. This colloquium was meant to be an important moment for dialogue, for addressing the other, in an attempt to go beyond the confusion that has led to the impasse in which the Islam-West relationship now finds itself.

The current critical international situation and the questions of life pressing on us brought relevancy to this colloquium, which was founded upon both meditative thought and hope. It was an appeal for a way of thinking, a culture, a reflection on the universal-to-come. Through peaceful words, it aimed to build bridges, to meet the other, in the goal of finding a way to face the unforseeability of the future together. On the methodological level, this colloquium was not limited to a series of doctrinal assertions or reminders about cultural heritages; it hoped, above all, to be a living dialogue between thinkers in the human and social sciences, on one of the essential themes of our times: "The dialogue between civilizations."

Through this colloquium, Algeria, an Arab-Berber country, African and Mediterranean, the closest to the West and therefore to France, had the measured hope of making the distance shorter and the abyss less profound. It is not by chance that the final encounter was devoted to Jacques Derrida: to us, he represented an ally of the highest level. This is why I wanted to write this book: so that the discussion it contains may continue to light our paths.

The Discussion

I was immediately struck by how many impressive people were in the audience. I welcomed them, making it clear that one doesn't introduce a master, one doesn't introduce Jacques Derrida. One welcomes him from the bottom of one's heart, respectfully, warmly, kindly, thanking him deeply for having accepted our invitation. I had been thinking for so long about this encounter, had been anticipating it, like something imperative, an act of faith, thinking of the questions I would bring up simply, through dialogue, with a major philosopher of our time, through a sharing of what is human, of what we have in common and which seems ungraspable, as "Algerians," and also, beyond all names and borders, in an attempt to confront briefly some of the many problems with which we are all faced today. The final session of our colloquium was not meant to be a classic philosophical exercise but above all a testimony to the fact that addressing the other is possible, that speech, respectful speech, thoughtful speech, frank speech, is the favored path to face up to our responsibilities. I also said that we mustn't take that word, "testimony," in a neutral way—quite the opposite. Testimony involves testifying, which is an act of faith, an involvement with the concrete in life, not only a theoretical or reflective act; for testimony, according to Derrida, is what goes beyond proof: to testify both to our commitment to the ideas we may share and to the expression of differences and divergences that can mark our difference, even if it is profound, as a richness. The future of civilizations, of cultures and religions, in short, the future of humanity, concerns us. It seems it is increasingly difficult to preserve roots and at the same time to carry out transformations, changes, and metamorphoses. Violence, the shrinking of the law, the absence of dialogue between worlds are among the disturbing realities we face. The fact that Jacques Derrida was with us is a strong sign that we must remain attached to the peaceful debates of ideas, without ever despairing. And so I simply said to him, welcome.

To Have Lived, and to Remember, as an Algerian

"Thank you. I would like to speak today as an Algerian," he responded with a smile. "I was born a Jew in Algeria, from that part of the community which in 1870 had obtained nationality through the Cremieux Decree, and then lost it in 1940. When I was ten years old, during the Vichy regime, I lost my French citizenship, and for a few years, unable to attend the French school, I was a member of what at the time was called the native Jews, who during those times experienced more support from the Algerians than from what were known as the Algerian French. That was one of the earth-shattering experiences of my existence, one of the earth-shattering Algerian experiences of my existence. There have been others. There was the war, of course, and there was what followed the war, all the symbolic and political earthquakes that have shaken Algeria since 1962, and which continue to shake it. Consequently, without overusing the rhetoric of the symbolic here, blending my compassion for the physical and psychic suffering of the Algerians today, who are suffering from the recent geological earthquake, I would like to focus my thoughts on the historical and political earthquake that has shaken Algeria and that continues to shake it, and which will continue, I suppose, unfortunately, to shake it for some time. These are a few of the heartfelt things I want to tell you. I want to speak here, today, as an Algerian, as an Algerian who became French at a given moment, lost his French citizenship, then recovered it. Of all the cultural wealth I have received, that I have inherited, my Algerian culture has sustained me the most. This is what I wanted to say as a testimony from the heart, before going on to the discussion that Mr. Chérif invited me to join."

I then asked him my first question concerning his experience and his vocation, his experience as an Algerian that he had just mentioned, which moved and touched us. I was eager to ask an initial question about that common past, especially given that in Algeria, including among the young generations, as complements to and in synthesis with our own Islamic and Arab-Berber values, we embrace, today as an independent people, our "Frenchness" and our "Mediterraneanness." We hope that, culturally speaking, that portion of "Algerianness," of Arabness and of Islamicity, within the framework of the Mediterranean dimension, will also be experienced in this way by France. I asked him, the fact that you are Algerian, of Algerian origin, that you grew up in Algerian culture, as a Franco-Maghrebin, Judeo-Arab Jew, did your experience, your proximity to and sharing with the other, the Muslim, on the Southern shores, contribute, in one way or another, to your philosophical orientation, to your vocation and work?

Without hesitation he replied, "The cultural heritage I received from Algeria is something that probably inspired my philosophical work. All the work I have pursued, with regard to European, Western, so-called Greco-European philosophical thought, the questions I have been led to ask from some distance, a certain exteriority, would certainly not have been possible if, in my personal history, I had not been a sort of child in the margins of Europe, a child of the Mediterranean, who was not simply French nor simply African, and who had passed his time traveling between one culture and the other feeding questions he asked himself out of that instability—all of which caused the earthquake of my experience that I just mentioned. Everything that has interested me for a long time, regarding writing, the trace, the deconstruction of Western metaphysics—which, despite what has been said, I have never identified as something homogeneous or defined in the singular (I have so often explicitly said the contrary)—all of that had to have come out of a reference to an elsewhere whose place and language were unknown or forbidden to me. Furthermore, in the middle of the war, right after the landing of the Allies in North Africa in November 1942, a sort of French literary capital in exile was formed in Algiers—there was a cultural effervescence, the presence of writers, a proliferation of journals and intellectual initiatives. This gave a visibility to Algerian literature of French expression, as we say, whether it involved writers of European origin, Camus and many others, or, a different movement, writers of Algerian origin. A few years later, in the still brilliant wake of this strange moment of glory, I was essentially harpooned by French literature and philosophy, at times both of them, at times one or the other. A Judeo-Franco-Maghrebin genealogy does not explain everything, far from it, but can I ever explain anything without it?"

Considering this very moving introspection, I asked further, how did you experience your relationship with the Arab language, Muslim culture, the Arab-Berber reality, and the history of Algeria within the framework of colonization, which implies a rejection of the dialogue of civilizations and a multiform violence exercised over the Algerian people?

He answered frankly and clearly: "The Arab language, that other, was unknown or forbidden to me by the established order. A ban was placed on the

Arab language. The ban took on many cultural and social forms for someone of my generation. But it was above all a school issue, something that happened at school, a pedagogical matter. The ban came out of an 'educational system,' as we say in France. Given the colonial censures and the social barriers, the various forms of racism, given the disappearance of Arabic as a daily, official, and administrative language, the only way to learn Arabic was at school, but as a foreign language; as that strange sort of foreign language that is the language of the other, although—and this is what is strange and disturbing—of an other who was the closest of the close. For me, Arabic was the language of the neighbor. Because I lived on the edge of an Arab neighborhood, on one of those borders that were both invisible and almost uncrossable: segregation was as effective as it was subtle. Before I disappeared into high school, there were still young Algerians. Close and infinitely far away—that was the distance that was inculcated into us, if I may say so, by experience. Unforgettable and universal. The optional study of Arabic was still of course allowed. We knew it was permitted, that is, everything except encouraged. The administration offered it in the same capacity and in the same form as the study of any other foreign language in all the French high schools in Algeria: Arabic—an optional foreign language in Algeria! The language taken away from us no doubt became the most foreign. Sometimes I wonder whether this language, unknown for me, is not my favorite language. The first of my preferred languages. And like each of my favorite languages, because I admit to having more than one, I like to hear it above all outside of any communication, in the poetic solemnity of song or prayer.

"As for Algerian history, we knew it from an obscure knowledge, Algeria being not at all the province of France, nor Algiers a popular neighborhood. For us, even as children, Algeria was also a country, Algiers a city in a country, in a distorted sense of that word. One could go on forever—some have already begun to do so here and there—in recounting what we were told, indeed, about the history of France, meaning by that what was taught in school under the name of the history of France, an unbelievable discipline, a fable and a bible, but a semipermanent indoctrination for the children of my generation: not a word about Algeria, not a single word about its history and its geography. The community to which I belonged was cut off in three ways: it was cut off first both from the Arab and the Berber, actually the Maghrebin language and culture; it was also cut off from the French, indeed European, language and culture, which were viewed as distant poles, unrelated to its history; and finally, or to begin with, it was cut off from the Jewish memory, from that history and that language that one must assume to be one's own, but which at a given moment no longer were—at least in a special way, for most of its members in a sufficiently living and internal way. The arrogant specificity, the traumatizing brutality of what is called the colonial war, colonial cruelty—some, including myself, experienced it from both sides, if I may say so."

East-West:
Unity and Differences

I could only add: one can easily imagine. In the same vein, and as an introduction to our discussion, to our common concerns, to the subject that brought us together, I attempted to explain that from my perspective, universal civilization belongs to everyone and is owned by no one. Every true civilization is pluralist, and every universal must be accessible to all. At the very least, one must recognize that the *Greek, Arab,* and *Jewish* peoples represented three major historical moments in the civilization of the Mediterranean basin. The West was Judeo-Islamo-Christian. Ancient Islam contributed to the development of modernity, and Islam's emancipatory force, beyond the deviations of some of its own followers today, makes it a natural participant in the search for new horizons. I asked

Derrida, and I asked myself at the same time, why do some people in the West still confine themselves in their construction of a simplistic notion of Islam and its culture and systematically contrast Eastern culture, which they consider "underdeveloped," to that of the West, which they view as "developed," according to their arbitrary criteria, and claim to be the only civilized ones, always seeking to impose their values through force? Is it reasonable to view our worlds as opposites? What is our responsibility today given our past and in the face of our future?

He interrupted me, smiling, and said, "These questions, as well as, I assume, those that follow, are too difficult and vast for me to respond directly and exhaustively. During our discussion, I'm going to try to find a way to follow your train of thought or at least to be a sounding board to reflect the spirit of the questions you ask. First of all, I do in fact believe that it is unfair to contrast cultures in that way; and what is more, it is unfair and unacceptable for anyone to attempt to impose his or her own vision and questionable political divisions through violence, whether colonial, imperial, or any other. I agree with you about the need to deconstruct the European intellectual construct of Islam. The so conventionally accepted contrast between Greeks, Jews, and Arabs must be challenged. We know very well that Arab thought and Greek thought intimately blended at a given historical moment and that one of the primary duties of our intellectual and philosophical memory is to rediscover that grafting, that reciprocal fertilization of the Greek, the Arab, and the Jew. Spain comes to mind. It so happens that my family was in Algeria before the colonization, and it probably came from the Spain where Greek, Arab, and Jewish thinking all intimately blended together. And I believe that one of our primary intellectual responsibilities today is to rediscover the sources and the moments in which those currents, far from being in contrast, truly fertilized each other. Further, I wouldn't contrast the East and the West, especially when talking about Algeria. First, the Arab and Muslim or Arabo-Muslim culture of Algeria and of Maghreb is also a Western culture. There are many Islams, there are many Wests."

I answered: there are indeed common aspects that some wish to deny and eliminate, but there are also differences between the Arabo-Muslim culture and the Judeo-Christian and Greco-Roman cultures, or any other culture in the world; they haven't followed the same path entirely, haven't had the same experience, regardless of their connections and similarities on many levels. Allow me to point out that, internally, despite appearances, our current and disturbing deviations, as well as our paralyzing sluggishness, not all Arabs/Muslims have the same problems, for example, with alterity, the universal, secularization, and secularism. In view of our history, this should go without saying, or in any case, pose fewer problems than for other cultural regions and for other religions. The contradictions and inconsistencies of certain archaic Arab regimes, on the one hand, and those of extremist politico-religious movements, on the other, as you know, are not Islam, and we are grateful for your exemplary objectivity. Beyond having aspects common to other monotheistic religions and, in the past, having also contributed to the benefit of universal civilization, contributions that we must value, preserve, and bring back to life, in our opinion, Islam is also fundamentally unique.

Consequently, what shocks us on the Southern shores is the fact that the dominant rationalist antireligious atheist discourse in the North makes inappropriate criticisms of and applies inadequate paradigms to Islam, like those applied to the history of Christianity, mythologies, and other beliefs. A certain West, even if it has contributed to some forms of emancipation, orders us to line up along a dehumanizing model, one that appears dual, like the face of Janus. This is an unbalanced and restrictive model, in our opinion, based on a strange a priori. To sum up, it sees itself as the only world to have chosen the rational function over the mythical dimension. That mythical dimension is associated with anything that is not on the order of strict rationalism. And that world is even more opposed to ways of life and values from the East, such as Islamic culture, which, in spite of the deviations of certain "Muslims" or of those who usurp that name, has however fully proven that it is capable of leading to what is true. Not only is there a complete lack of understanding—Islam truly appears as an unknown—but what is more, modern reason has serious difficulty explaining and resolving the question of life's struggles: Who are we? What are we destined for, why are we put to the test on earth? How can we learn to live, notably within the framework of a life without religion? The fact that the modern world speaks, for example, of nature, of objective facts, of a cosmos without cause or a goal, instead of a world created, ordered, filled with visible and invisible signs, does not bother us too much. Today, we, like the insurgents, are above all shocked, profoundly disappointed to see that a revolution, indeed the revolutions, the promises of progress, have been transformed into threats, into dehumanization, and that at the same time our version of what is human is ignored.

If we hazard to criticize, however peacefully, however naturally, the deviations, the lies, the duplicity, the confusion, the law of the strongest, the perversions of some practices of freedom, all doors close, and we are accused of every evil. However, at the same time, we criticize our own contradictions as well, those of our own people who react irrationally, darkly, and absurdly to the politics of double standards, to hypocritical political discourse, to the refusal of dialogue and negotiation. The shameless exploitation of these blind reactions, to discredit the other and continue to refuse dialogue and justice, is devastating. We demand the universalism of democracy, dialogue, and negotiations in the common interest; because we know we are all in the same boat, all caught up in the same movement. Our hope is democracy at the level of international relations; it decisively determines internal situations and relations between peoples, beyond their specific differences. Where, then, are universal democracy and dialogue, words that so many of those in power repeat ad nauseam?

Derrida answered me gently, but quite firmly: "What you call the universalism of democracy, a concept that is very difficult to define, presupposes that democracy is conceived in a way other than as a fixed model of a political regime. I believe that what distinguishes the idea of democracy from all other ideas of political regimes—monarchy, aristocracy, oligarchy, and so on—is that democracy is the only political system, a model without a model, that accepts its own historicity, that is, its own future, which accepts its self-criticism, which accepts its perfectibility. You are correct: it is your democratic right to criticize the insufficiencies, the contradictions, the imperfections of our systems. To exist in a democracy is to agree to challenge, to be challenged, to challenge the status quo, which is called democratic, in the name of a democracy to come. This is why I always speak of a democracy to come. Democracy is always to come, it is a promise, and it is in the name of that promise that one can always criticize, question that which is proposed as de facto democracy. Consequently, I believe that there doesn't exist in the world a democracy suitable for the concept of the democracy to come. And consequently, if there is to be dialogue, since you speak of the absence of dialogue, it can only occur in the revelation of that democracy to come, whose occurrence and promise remain before us. That occurrence and promise enable us, at every moment, to criticize. A democracy is a social organization in which every citizen has the right to criticize, in the name of democracy, the state of things that are called democratic. This is how one recognizes a democracy: the right to say everything, the right to criticize the allegation, or the so-called democracy, in the name of a democracy to come.

"The concept of democracy, the word, originate in Greek culture, no one can deny this. And it is not to be Grecocentric or Eurocentric to say so; the word comes from Greek culture. But from the beginning, Greek culture associated the concept of democracy with concepts from which, today, the democracy to come is attempting to free itself: the concept of autochthony, that is, the concept of being born on a land and belonging to it through birth, the concept of territory, the very concept of State. I have nothing against the State, I have nothing against citizenship,

but I dare to dream of a democracy that is not simply tied to a nation-state and to citizenship. And it is
under these conditions that one can speak of a universal democracy, a democracy that is not only cosmopolitical but universal. Granted, cosmopolitanism is a
very respectable notion, but it is nevertheless associated with the notion of State and of politics linked
to the polis as nation-state and territoriality. Beyond
all cosmopolitanisms, there is a universal democracy,
which goes well beyond citizenship and the nation-
state. Therefore, I believe that if a dialogue is to be
opened between what you call the West and the East,
between the different cultural regions and the different religious regions of the world, if such an exchange
is possible through words, through thoughts, and not
through force, if such a dialogue and exchange are
possible without resorting to force, they must occur
on the horizon of that democracy to come, which is
not connected to a nation-state, which is not connected to citizenship, to territoriality. That is the
condition for free speech, for an exchange, for what
you call a dialogue. I don't use the word 'dialogue'
very much—its sometimes exploitive connotations
are well known. I would call it 'speech addressed to
the other recognized as other, recognized in his alterity.' This speech addressed to the other presupposes
the freedom to say anything, on the horizon of a democracy to come that is not connected to the nation,
the State, religion, which is not even connected to

language. Naturally, the religion of the other must be recognized and respected, as well as his mother tongue, of course. But one must translate, that is, at the same time respect the language of the other and, through that respect, get his meaning across, and this presupposes what you have called a universal democracy. Yes, through that respect, getting the meaning across, this presupposes a universal democracy, that is, a democracy beyond the sovereignties of national, territorial States, beyond territorialities, and using all the new technologies that in fact enable us to go beyond the territorial limits of communication, that open up onto a new international law. To achieve this, I believe we need a new international law. For what you have called dialogue to be possible, without constraints, without the use of force, we need a truly international law, renovated and respected international institutions capable of imposing their decisions. You know very well that the crises we are experiencing are above all crises of international law, crises of sovereignty linked both to the loss of sovereignty of small States and to the abuse of the sovereignty of powerful States. I place the issue of the sovereignty of the nation-state at the heart of our discussion, and I believe that if what you call the universalism of democracy is to make possible what you call dialogue, which is lacking today, that will occur only through the creation of a new international law."

Injustice and Decline

I wanted to share my concern with him. As intellectuals, and even simply as human beings, we are worried; we note that the modern world, to which, by the way, we aspire, seems marked by a certain number of negative tendencies. We do recognize that on the Southern shores there is resistance to change, a refusal to come to agreement, deviations in other forms, such as a withdrawal, whether in a political, social, or cultural sense. Sometimes it is a matter of rearguard battles. We must accept evolution, but I believe we have the right to oppose the hegemony of a model that is unjust. Globally, we don't have the choice, modernity is inevitable, but we have the duty to criticize and to attempt to correct, to rectify, and to adapt that which appears to us to be contrary to our interests and values. We must assume the demands of the universal without at the same time losing our bearings. What is at stake is essential.

How can we be modern without losing our roots? Consequently, how can we undertake development under the universal world model and be vigilant vis-à-vis a certain number of pitfalls of rationalism, the result of what we call, in economics, neoliberalism, or the domination of profit for profit that destroys the principle of justice; and then, on the level of meaning, how do we deal with *the removal of religion from life*, or at the very least the end of morality as it has been bequeathed by monotheism, a situation that destroys ethics and identity?

Modernity encourages the primacy of reason, secularity, and frees energies: this is a positive thing. But at least three of its tendencies seem to me to demand responses, corrections, and alternatives, because they are marked by imbalances, contrasts of levels that are fatal for human equilibrium, in contrast to Islam, which instead seeks connections, coherence, and balance, without confusing the different levels and spheres of life. *On the level of meaning,* the disturbing point is moral. There are fewer and fewer connections between the concept of the modern citizen and the horizon toward which monotheistic peoples in general, and Muslims in particular, are reaching. It is not the end of the world, but the end of a world.

How can we invent another world that rejects all closure and idolatry, while connecting to the temporal and the spiritual within it? Apparently, today, modernity is not simply secularization, which Derrida rightly recommends, but dehumanization, despiritualization, *de-signification*.

On the political level, the social body, under the yoke of capitalism, is responsible for executing policy. This depoliticization, in our opinion, is unprecedented: it challenges the possibility of making history, of being a responsible people. In the developed world, in spite of debates, the legitimacy of institutions, the predominance of human rights, the possibility of existing as responsible citizens, participating in the collective and public quest for the just, the beautiful, and the true, seems increasingly problematic. We have no political existence in either the modern or in the Abrahamic sense. This situation is worsened by the bellicose acts of the powerful and the suicidal acts of the weak. *On the level of knowledge,* in our opinion, we are witnessing a challenge to the possibility of thinking, and of thinking in a different way. Globalization aims to master everything through the use of the exact sciences, which are alone considered able to aid in development, which is of course a kind of scientism. The reduction of the ability to assume the intercultural and interdisciplinarity and the problems that arise when nature is manipulated are reflections of this.

Consequently, I asked Derrida about a concise formula: the triptych "secularism, scientism, capitalism," which is the emblem of the modern West, seems to us to be a source of imbalance and of serious problems—how should we face them?

"Let me focus," he said, "on those three words in your question that you have associated in what you call the Western triptych; I don't know whether it is a Western triptych, but in any case I will look at those three words, I will reconnect those three words: scientism, laicism, capitalism. First, scientism is a detestable thing; it isn't knowledge, the realm of scholars, men of science. Scientific practice is always devoid of scientism. Scientism is the positivist allegation of scientific power; it is not knowledge and science. Therefore, scientism is always a bad thing. As for secularism, however, I believe that at present it is calling for its own transformation, and I believe that this is occurring in France today. I believe that the democracy to come, which I talked about earlier, assumes secularism, that is, both the detachment of the political from the theocratic and the theological, thus entailing a certain secularism of the political, while at the same time, encompassing freedom of worship in a completely consistent, coherent way, and absolute religious freedom guaranteed by the State, on the condition, obviously, that the secular space of the political and the religious space are not confused. I believe that today we need a concept of the secular that no longer has that sort of aggressive compulsion that it once had in France, in the moments of crisis between the State and religion. I believe that the secular today must be more rigorous with itself, more tolerant toward religious cultures and toward the possibility for religious practices to exist freely, unequivocally, and without confusion. Of course, the autonomous individual, in a society, I am not sure I know very well what that is. The autonomous individual is a subject who gives himself or herself his or her law, a sovereign subject: here again I would be tempted to suggest that the freedom of such an individual also presupposes a certain heteronomy, that is, a certain acceptance of the law of the other. The law is always the law of the other, in a certain sense. But this heteronomy does not presuppose servitude or subjugation, and the religious community can very well organize itself as a religious community, in a lay space, without invading the lay space and while respecting the freedom of the individual. In other words, personally—but perhaps I am translating a personal idiosyncrasy here—I have always had the tendency to resist religious communitarianism, that is, any form of gregarious community that oppresses the individual, that prevents the individual from acting as a nonreligious citizen. One can be religious, of course, and yet act as a lay citizen, without feeling herded by a religious community.

"You speak about the connections between the two levels. It is very difficult to connect the conundrum in which France is involved today—but not just France. The problem is one of finding a connection that is as peaceful as possible between the freedom of the individual or the citizen and his or her belonging to a religious community, provided that his or her belonging to the religious community is not oppressive, overwhelming, or repressive. And I believe in the responsibility of the State, because everything I said before on the subject of the decline or the crisis of the sovereign nation-state does not prevent me from thinking that we need the State, and I am not against the State. I ask questions about the sovereignty of the State and about its origin, which is itself theological, by the way. I believe that the concepts of the political on which we live are secularized theological concepts; thus I ask myself questions about the religious origins of the idea of sovereignty and even about the idea of the State. But in asking these questions, I am not wholesale rejecting the need for the State. The State, under certain conditions—and it is these conditions that must be evaluated each time, it is in these conditions that one must assume one's responsibilities—the State may be the guarantor of secularity, or of the life of religious communities. The State can oppose economic forces, abusive economic concentrations, international forces of economic powers. Consequently, I believe that the State is not bad in itself, even if one must constantly question its sovereignty, its fundamentally theological origins, and this is the difficulty, what I call deconstruction, namely, to do these two things at the same time: to ask questions, for example, about the theological genealogy of the concepts of the political that organize Western thought, and European thought in particular, on the one hand, and, on the other, to maintain, in determined and determinable contexts, the survival of those concepts that one is in the process of questioning and deconstructing.

Obviously, we are not going to avoid the questions we are all thinking of here, the questions that are raised between, let's say, the West, what we call the West, a notion that we must also divide—the European West is not the American West—and the East, which must also be divided, which is not simply the Arab-Muslim world. Nevertheless, with regard to these questions, I believe that the condition of what you have called dialogue, of the speech addressed to the other without violence, is the common acceptance of the democracy to come that I mentioned earlier, which presupposes deconstruction, the deconstructive question raised on the subject of the sovereignty of the nation-state, the authentic secularization of the political, that is, the separation between the theocratic and the political. I believe that we must—here I am speaking as a Frenchman, a Westerner, a Western philosopher—I believe that what we must consider as our first task is to *ally* ourselves to that in the Arab and Muslim world which is trying to advance the idea of a secularization of the political, the idea of a separation between the theocratic and the political—this both out of respect for the political and for democratization and out of respect for faith and religion. On both sides we have much to win from the dissociation between the theocratic and the political. This, and it goes without saying, presupposes a transformation of the concept of the political; in particular, it presupposes a questioning of what I have called the secularization of that concept of the political that remains among the most fundamental concepts of the so-called European political thought, which is fundamentally theological."

Separation or Connection?

I felt, and feel the problematic is still relevant, that pursuing a knowledge of the other is essential, given the difficulty of learning how to live, given the injustices, failures, impasses, or negative tendencies both of modern reason and of churches. It is essential for us Muslims, as well, given the awareness that fundamentally existence is presented, on the one hand, in the form of the Mystery, of the Open that is always out of reach, is hiding and asks to be assumed as such, and, on the other hand, in the form of the incontrovertible relationship between unity and plurality, two dimensions strengthened by many major beliefs that resonate deeply in the memory of Muslims. Some people in the West feel there is no possibility of coherence, no possible connection, no communication between the essential levels, the spiritual sense, and those of logic and justice. But Islam wants engagement with regard to the Mystery, loyalty to the revealed Message, and a specific attachment to the religious vision that the last life is the final aim. This doesn't prevent it from distinguishing between religion and politics, while being careful, as I have said, not to confuse those two dimensions and also to engage the direction of the century, a realm in which today it is delayed or even worse, appears antimodern because some of its own instrumentalize religion and lapse into intolerance. Beyond these contradictions, deviations, and negative facts, and the positive fact that Islam does not neglect earthly matters (without the sky crushing the earth), the relationship to the Mystery remains at the heart of the Muslim's faith. I knew that this point was a point of difference, and I formulated my question in this way: what can philosophy say today on the subject of the Mystery?

Smiling broadly, Derrida said, "When I was a student, following the tradition of Gabriel Marcel, we often distinguished between the Mystery and the problem, the problem being the object of a philosophical development, and the Mystery being that which cannot be turned into a problem. But I am not going to go into this story of the concept of Mystery and problem. I will say the following: Mystery encompasses everything that involves that which in life is still unknown to us, both in the sense that science still has discoveries to make, that science has progress to make, in its knowledge of life, genetics, biology, and also in the sense of life as existence. I believe that the secularization of the political, that is, the separation between the political and the theocratic, will not be harmful at all; if anything, it will enable a deeper questioning of what you have called the Mystery of life and of issues regarding faith. Personally, I always distinguish between faith and religion. I believe that there are many religions, positive religions, to which one can belong or not belong; there are religions that I call Abrahamic that are the Jewish religion, the Christian religion, the Muslim religion, with their common foundation or "trunk." There are other cultures that one calls religious and that are not perhaps religions. The concept of religion is an obscure concept. In *Faith and Knowledge*, I attempted to write on this subject, on the obscurity of the very concept of religion. Is Buddhism a religion? Is Taoism a religion? These are essential questions that we cannot address here. For the moment, if we limit ourselves to what we have customarily called religion in the Abrahamic universe of the religions of the Book, I will then distinguish between the religious adherences to Judaism, Christianity, and Islam and faith without which no social relationship is possible. I cannot address the other, whoever he or she might be, regardless of his or her religion, language, culture, without asking that other to believe me and to trust me. One's relationship to the other, addressing the other, presupposes faith. One can never show, one can never prove that someone is or isn't lying—it is impossible to prove. One can always say: I said something that is false, but I said it sincerely; I was mistaken, but I wasn't lying. Consequently, when someone is speaking to us, he or she is asking to be believed. And that belief assures both the exchange of words and financial credit, social credit, and all forms of credit and legitimacy in society. This faith is the condition of the social bond itself. There is no social bond without faith. Now, I believe that one can radicalize the secularization of the political while maintaining this necessity for faith in the general sense that I have just defined and then, on the foundation of this universal faith, this shared faith, this faith without which there is no social bond, one can and one must respect strictly defined religious affiliations. And I am persuaded that authentic believers, those who are truly Jewish, Christian, or Muslim, those who are truly living their religious beliefs and not simply endorsing the dogma of those religions, are more ready to understand the religion of the other and to accede to that faith, whose universal structure I have just described, than others. Consequently, I believe there is no contradiction between political secularization and a relationship to what you call the Mystery of life, that is, the fact of living together in faith. The act of faith is not a miraculous thing; it is the air that we breathe. As soon as I start to speak, even if I am lying, I am telling you:

I am telling you the truth, believe me, I promise to tell you the truth. And this act of faith is implied in the social relationship, in the social bond itself; I am persuaded that authentic believers, those who are not what one calls fundamentalists, dogmatists ready to transform their belief into weapons of war, those who are not dogmatic and fundamentalist are more ready to understand the religion of the other and universal faith. Consequently, I believe that far from there being a contradiction, there is a connection between the secularization of the political, the dissociation, in a sense, of the social bond, from the political bond, and what you call the relationship to the Mystery of life."

I then refocused my question on our harsh reality: how can we reestablish dialogue between worlds? While it is an opening up that must dominate, how can we confront the forces of closure in order to face the common challenges and the complexity of our history?

He replied: "An opening up is something that is decided. One cannot force someone to speak or to listen; this is where the question of faith returns. An opening up must occur where there is war, and there is war everywhere in the world today. Peace is only possible when one of the warring sides takes the first step, the hazardous initiative, the risk of opening up dialogue, and decides to make the gesture that will lead not only to an armistice but to peace. The difference between armistice and peace is that an armistice temporarily brings a warring situation to an end, whereas peace, as Kant said, is perpetual, peace is essentially perpetual. The concept of peace implies perpetuity. One doesn't stop war for a moment, one commits to peace forever. I am thinking here of the ongoing wars in the Middle East, I am thinking of Israel and Palestine, and I am also thinking of the more or less virtual wars. I could give a thousand examples, unfortunately, too many examples of wars; in each instance, the difference between an opening up and a closure depends on the risk taken, on the responsibility taken in the midst of risk, by someone who knows that, if he is not the first to address the other, if he is not the first to offer his hand, the war will not end. If one waits, if one always places a precondition on the ceasing of hostilities, then there will be perpetual war. The difference between closure and opening up is the question of responsibility, isn't it? I must say yes to the other, and that yes to the other is an initiative. When you say yes, it is a free gesture, it is an absolute initiative, but it is already a response. When I say yes, the structure of the yes is the structure of a response. When you say yes, you begin by responding. If someone, let's say a head of State from the Middle East, says yes to peace first, taking the risks he must take in that case, it is the question of the opening up that will make possible reconciliation, negotiation, the establishment of peace. Thus opening up and closure are not imposed from outside, one must take the risk of the yes, that is, of the inherent affirmation of life."

Concerned with opening up, but critical with regard to the vicissitudes of modernity, I said, whereas it is very difficult to learn how to live, and there is no convincing model, rather only disappointing and worrying ones, why this aggressiveness toward Islam, why must we all be Westernized, Europeanized, Americanized, to conform to progress, and thus appear to be civilized?

This eminent philosopher, who was speaking to me with so much attention and erudite passion, told me with humility and conviction, "Here, too, you are asking me a very difficult question, which like all of your questions begs very long answers, and I'm a bit ashamed to improvise such simplified responses. One can say in a certain sense that what is often erroneously termed *mondialisation* in French, or "globalization," as the Americans call it, has been a universal Europeanization through science and technology, and even those who oppose this Europeanization, even those who, through acts of terrorist violence, claim to oppose this violent Europeanization, this violent Americanization, do so most often using a certain technical, techno-scientific, sometimes techno-economic-scientific Europeanization. Therefore, I believe we must again look at concepts thoroughly. First, I believe that, paradoxically, globalization hasn't occurred. It is a false concept, often an alibi; never has the world been so unequal and so marginally shareable or shared. Further, I believe that it is time to distinguish between Americanization and Europeanization, since you have spoken of Americanization and Europeanization. Those who know my work, and forgive me for referring to it, know that I do not claim to be Eurocentric, rather I claim to be someone who has questioned Eurocentrism. Nevertheless, I believe that we are at a moment in history, we have been for some time and in particular within the last few months, when the division between a certain America—I'm not speaking of the United States in general, but of a certain American power, a certain American politics—the division between a certain American politics and a virtuality of European politics is increasingly possible. Once again, without Eurocentrism, I believe that it falls to, or that it should fall to, a certain Europe that is in the process of creating itself, to take on new responsibilities, both to differentiate itself, to break away from a certain hegemonic unilateralism of the United States, and to engage those forces in the world, in the Arab-Muslim world, that are in turn ready to open up to the democracy to come that I mentioned earlier. For me, this is something new.

"Once again, in my work I have a tendency to beware of Eurocentric traditions, not only colonialist, of course, but Eurocentric in the structure of concepts that have founded international law. The law of the UN, the Security Council, are founded on Western concepts, and I have a tendency to challenge that. Nevertheless, from what occurred at the first signs of the war, of the aggression against Iraq (it goes without saying that like many of us here, I have no sympathy for the regime that has just collapsed in Iraq, but I was very strongly opposed to the way in which the United States led this affair, unilaterally, in violation of UN laws and of those of the Security Council), well, I believe, and this will be repeated in an article that I am going to sign with the German philosopher Habermas that will be published in the newspaper *Libération* at the end of the month, I believe that there have recently been important dates when such and such a European minister, I'm thinking of Aznar, Berlusconi, Blair, have attempted to drag all of Europe behind the United States and, at the same time, massive popular demonstrations in the streets of those same countries and other countries against the American initiative. We have here, and in the joint gesture of France and Germany, the first signs of a type of Europe that, far from wanting to Europeanize the world, could step between the hegemony of the American superpower (itself precarious, itself criticized, because this hegemony is very powerful and at the same time shows signs of weakness, which is not contradictory) and the rest of the world and commit to a dialogue, to repeat your word, with nation-states or Arab-Muslim cultures in the spirit of the democracy to come that I mentioned earlier. I believe that there is a new European responsibility that is being sought today and for which I am cheering. I have tried to say this better elsewhere, in the little book called *Voyous*, or in the text I mentioned. To say it very simply, I believe that today we must abandon the idea that there is a Europeanization, a violent hegemony of a West that includes the United States and Europe against the rest of the world. I believe we must abandon this idea. There is a specificity of a Europe in formation, which I hope, along with many countries of the Mediterranean basin, notably the countries of Maghreb and specifically Algeria, but also the countries of the Middle East, will transform the world configuration in which we live, and this in the spirit of that democracy to come of which I am speaking a bit much this evening, but it is an economical term which I am forced to use to go quickly."

At that precise moment I thanked him, as if to tell him the message was well received. Then I added, despite the specificities of each entity and the differences between Europe and America, why does this dominant world find it so difficult to assume its responsibilities through a kind of meditative thought, which does not despise religion but, instead, favors the resolution of political questions still open in the world as well as the solution of problems of justice?

For us, it appears that the West, the motor of modernity, does not propose a strong politics, nor a project for a society in which the question of justice, on the one hand, and that of meaning, on the other, are central. What, then, are the interest, strength, and specificity of this European model that ignores or marginalizes, indeed criticizes and battles everything that is religious and every link between the spiritual and the temporal?

Derrida answered, saying, "You see, I believe that Europe is a confused concept and a common name for very diverse things: the relationship of the State to religion is not the same in France, Germany, England, Italy, and nevertheless, there is something common to all the European States, which is a certain principle of separation between the State and religion, without scorn for religion. By contrast, in the United States and in certain Arab-Muslim States, there is, on the contrary, in different forms on either side, very often merging or an alliance between politics and the theocratic, which, today, we must, in my opinion, question and transform. And the meditative thought that you invoke should address these points. And I believe that it is not at all a comment against religion to say this; on the contrary, it is out of respect for religion that we must dissociate things and that we must cease to lead politics in the name of religion, or under the authority of religion, or sometimes under the authority of religious authorities themselves. What unfortunately a given American head of State and another head of State of an Arab and Muslim country have in common is that their political discourse is a religious discourse in its most dogmatic form. I have never believed that it is possible to synthesize the existence of any individual, in any case not my own, and therefore I believe that dissociation is inescapable. The social relationship is also made of interruption. To relate to the other, as other, is not simply to be linked to the other; it is also to respect the interruption. The relationship as our relationships, as Blanchot or Levinas said. To relate to the other presupposes faith. Nevertheless, even if one recognizes this insurmountable dissociation in each of us and between us, to live together is also to recognize the dissociation and interruption. With regard to the question of what you call the globality or the totality of the human being: I believe that it is possible to live or to attempt to live this totality, even to live it religiously, or to make religion the principle of this unification. This is not my case, but I easily admit that it can be the case for someone else, someone who finds not only in faith in general but in a given religious faith the principle of a global unity for his or her behavior, ethics, rule of life, without having to turn it into a system of political rules to be universalized and imposed on others. I believe that the sphere of the political, or the sphere of law, and thus also that of justice (I distinguish law from justice) must be separated from this globality of human existence. I do not believe that the attention paid to a certain totality of existence, a globality of oneself, implies totalitarianism, the sort of totalization of the model of this existence as a political model. I believe that the relationship to the other is the condition for justice. I always distinguish law from justice: law has a history, which is inadequate for justice; there are laws, and if a given body of law has a history, it is precisely because what is just is not always reduced to the law, to the juridical, to the legal. I believe that the sense of justice that can inspire us in our existence must not be reduced to the juridical, nor should it be identified with the political. Here, too, I am for the dissociation between the different spheres of the political, the juridical, and the existential."

I then brought up the issue of globalization, which concerns us on the Southern shores. The marginalization of spiritual values, the weakening of the possibility of being a responsible citizen, extreme permissiveness and, in reaction to it, a fundamentalism of bans and their exploitation for illegitimate ends, and above all, the impoverishment of most of humanity, as Derrida so rightly said in *Specters of Marx:* "Never have violence, inequality, exclusion, famine, and thus economic oppression affected so many people on the earth, so much of humanity"—is all of that irreversible, given the egoism and the blindness of certain decision makers in the North and given the paralysis of others in the South, frightened by the idea of change and transparency? In the North people sometimes speak of solidarity, but we note few changes in reality. Aids to development are reduced and represent on average a miserable 0.2 percent of the budget of rich countries, 0.1 percent in the United States, and the financial and economic policies of international institutions do not take into account the objectives of independence, the specificities, and the dignity of human beings. For dozens of countries, the Third World has become a Fourth World, and poverty there has become extreme poverty. For a third to a quarter, it is almost a Zero World, a sort of "absence of world" people that we have before our eyes. The gap between rich and poor countries sometimes reaches a difference of one to ten, which makes them often incomparable, as in some poor countries, there isn't access even to potable water, a minimal amount of food, or the slightest possibility of health care. In the North, we witness the creation of wealth and policies followed by societies of unlimited consumption, without any control over their needs. In the South, we experience the impoverishment of many populations deprived of the conditions of even a decent life, sometimes confronted with the harshness of nature and often with exploitation, pillaging, and domination, either direct or indirect, internal and external. This leads to harmful imbalances, to inequalities and fractures, and reinforces the law of the strongest, while at the same time we hear of globalization, human rights, and democracy. This reduces or destroys all faith in discourses promoting the capitalist model and globalization. The least one can say is that the relations between countries are feebly marked by the democratic spirit, at least as the founding fathers of the UN charter and of the Universal Declaration of Human Rights had imagined it. A fact that, obviously, does not prevent us from taking resolutely the path that will lead there. To commit to a universal democratic ideal and want at the same time to be inspired by Islam is our right; justice and meaning are our demands, knowing that we must accept the idea that nothing is given in advance and that there is no preestablished path to follow. The path to democracy, which is lacking in both our societies, especially in the South, and at the level of international relations, in our humble opinion, must engage an infinite will for coexistence and respect for the other. It is imperative to reach an international democracy in order to reconstruct just relations between individuals, on the one hand, and between societies, on the other. One cannot happen without the other. And yet we are forced, in vain, to envision perspectives that are foreign to our specific cultures, and in addition, that have not been proven. Consequently, I said to my guest: in *Specters of Marx* and your last work entitled *Voyous*, a significant title in view of the current world disorder, you say something that calls upon us and interests us to the highest degree, we others, on the

Southern shores, who are committed to finding an alternative.

He replied: "Indeed, the context in which I said those things concerned the concept of globalization, which is often put forth through questionable rhetoric, to make us believe that everyone has free access not only to technology and to means of communication but also to the wealth of the world, that the markets are open, that the States themselves no longer make the laws. This concept of globalization belongs to an opaque rhetoric that leads us to believe that transparency and equality are not only in the works but have already occurred. In *Specters of Marx,* I analyze what I call the ten wounds of the world order; never like today, in absolute numbers, has there been so much inequality, famine, misery, underemployment, people who don't have work where they need to, people who work too much where they should work less. Never has there been so much injustice. What is thus called for in this situation, which is everything except globalizing, is a transformation of international law, a transformation of the relationships of sovereignty, a technical, economic, and political transformation. I do not wish to bring everything always back to questions of law, since I alluded more than once already to international law, to the UN, to the Security Council. Nevertheless, I believe that, at the moment when the events we have just experienced, that we are now experiencing, occur in a spectacular, dramatic way, through scenes violating international law, we must recognize that international institutions are not what they should be, because they are powerless, because they are structured by concepts of European origin that must be reconsidered and perfected. I am not against the UN; I am for the perfectability of the UN. And above all, one sees that it is an institution that has no means of its own to ensure the application of its decisions, to put its own decisions into action. That means that each time the UN, or the Security Council, makes a decision, they have to defer the application, the execution of it to the most militarily, economically, technically powerful State, which for the most part is the United States, which has the power to decree that a given State is a rogue state. Well, it is this situation that must be changed, which is changing profoundly, in the midst of suffering, pain, indetermination, with a thousand unknowns before us. This situation must change first from the juridical point of view. I am not an orthodox Marxist, but ultimately, I know well that the juridical structures are formal structures carried by infrastructural conditions, which are of a techno-economic type. What must be transformed is the relationship among these techno-economic forces, which itself will transform the juridical relationships and will put into place new international institutions, a new sharing of sovereignty, a new concept of sovereignty. The concept of sovereignty that comes to us with a theological heritage presupposes indivisibility. All the great theoreticians of sovereignty, whether it is Bodin or Hobbes, proposed, and no one up to now has questioned this definition, that sovereignty is indivisible, whether it be that of the monarch, the people, or the individual. Today, we must take into account the fact that sovereignty is to be shared, that it is divisible. There is no longer any pure sovereignty; there is no longer a pure sovereign nation-state. The world must therefore be reorganized so that new divisions of sovereignty are put into place and so that relationships of techno-economic force enable this transformation of the law and of sovereignty. This passes through democracy, through the people, through each people's capacity to embrace democracy, to organize democracy while contesting, each in his or her place, each from his or her situation and unique context, the theocratic authority that mutilates or subjugates democracy in any way.

"It is essential that everywhere, and I am not just speaking of the Arab and Muslim, or Arab-Muslim world, I am also speaking of Europe and the United States and South America, that people take responsibility for this democratization; in order to do this, they have to become committed to the secularization of the political, without the need to renounce faith or religion. I do not believe that the secularization of the political presupposes a denial of religion. On the contrary, I believe that authentic believers, if that word has a meaning, are the first, or should be the first, to demand the separation of the political and the religious, because this is also the condition for the freedom of religion. It is the condition that enables the State to guarantee freedom of religion, so that religious communities can live according to their wishes and their desires. Therefore, I believe that we have to constitute new alliances between these new Europeans about whom I spoke earlier and certain Americans (I don't want to put all Americans in the same boat; when I speak of America, I am speaking of the America of Bush), certain Britons, certain Arab citizens, certain Muslims, Berbers, non-Christians, non-Jews. In *Specters of Marx,* I speak of a new international alliance, not of a new international, as it was the case in Marxist language, but of a new international that allies, beyond citizenship, thus beyond States, all people who wish to change the world in the direction we have just indicated. And there are signs of this alliance, the movement that we call anti-globalization, a movement that is itself heterogeneous but the bearer of certain symptoms, of signs that men and women from all countries can unite in struggles against political, economic, and religious practices that must be fought. I believe in these new international alliances. They are still weak, they are nascent, heterogeneous, they are seeking each other out, but I am sure that they exist. We have signs that they are seeking each other out. The philosopher Kant said that, sometimes, even through failures—for example, that of the French Republic (he was for the French Republic, but he considered it a failure at the moment of the Terror)—even through the failure of an enterprise that could have been worthy and noble, we have the sign—he said commemorative or annunciative, anticipating—the sign that progress is possible, that a perfectibility is coming. Well, I believe that in all movements of antiglobalization today, all the movements that bring together so many men and women against economic violence, against terrorist violence, against State violence, against all the imperial and imperialist hegemonies, there is the sign of a new alliance that is forming. And my wish, today, is that not only Europeans and Americans participate in that alliance but also Algerians, Tunisians, Moroccans—Muslims from all the Arab-Muslim and Muslim nations. Each one naturally cannot do so and must not do so except as an Algerian, or as a Morrocan, or as an Iraqi, a Saudi, each one in his unique situation. A French person cannot do it as an Algerian, cannot do it as a Morrocan; each one, in his situation, must assume his or her responsibilities. You asked me earlier how to open and not close democracy: one must take the initiative for it. It is not something that is imported or exported; one doesn't parachute democracy in. Democracy cannot be imposed on Iraq by force. We know very well what threatens to happen: other religious powers threaten to take democracy in hand, to appropriate it in turn, to confiscate it, and to achieve the opposite result from that which is sought. I remember, for example, that terrible moment of the threat of confiscation of democracy by the Islamist movement, when it was necessary, in Algeria, to suspend elections. I don't want to discuss that here, we don't have time, and it deserves a lengthy analysis. Elections were suspended due to or on the pretext that enemies of democracy were going to take power. And then there were terrible responsibilities to take on. Even in the face of a situation in which, sometimes, in the name of democracy, the enemies of democracy can seize it, the responsibilities are unique, they are terrible: for in this case one takes responsibility not knowing where one is. And yet, if one knew what one should do, if knowledge could simply guide our action, there wouldn't be any responsibility. We know what must be done, we do it, and there's no responsibility, no decision to be made. Responsibility, decisions, are taken in the darkness that is the lack of knowledge, which doesn't mean we must cultivate ignorance, lack of knowledge, obscurantism. We must know. One must accumulate the most knowledge and critical awareness possible. One must be for scientific knowledge, science, as far as possible, not for scientism. But we must also know that the moment of decision, the moment of responsibility, the moment of opening up, does not come out of knowledge. It is a leap that must be made by each person wherever he or she is and in the unique situation in which he or she happens to be. Between knowledge and responsibility there is an abyss. Thus we must have knowledge. We need knowledge, we must cultivate science, but science alone is not enough. We know very well that the most violent movements today, the movements we call terrorist, are often associated with techno-scientific modernity. Knowledge guarantees neither democracy nor moral responsibility nor justice. Thus we must have knowledge, one must reject neither knowledge nor critical awareness, but there are also moments of faith, in which a leap is made, the leap of opening up, toward that new alliance that I mentioned earlier."

Progress Is Absolute, or There Is No Progress

At that precise moment when he was talking about alliance (a subject I hold very dear) in order to achieve progress while maintaining distinctiveness, I decided to raise the key question of the relationship between authenticity and progress.

On a cultural level, we know that an identity is never fixed. It is the expression of a relationship to time, space, and values. Even more than others, I think, we Muslims try to connect what may be called perennial values with evolutionary values, authenticity therefore with modernity; this is our concern and our challenge. Spiritual values and the exercise of critical reason must allow us to remain open in our relationships with the other, the world and memory, the meaning of becoming, life, and death. We still have many things to do; the path is long.

All the same, Algeria, for example, which occupies a favored geostrategic position as a crossroads and which has always paid a high price for its freedom, an Arab and Muslim country that is also Mediterranean, and which has lost many of its taboos, is capable of achieving the so hoped-for synthesis of the modern and the authentic. Today, we want to assert our Mediterraneanness, our global perspective, while being careful not to lose a certain number of those bearings linked to our sources, to our historical and civilizational heritage. No civilization or society can live in autarchy, in closure; and our texts not only authorize but demand the welcoming and respect of the different other. This is why we are fundamentally attached to hospitality, to exchanges, to negotiation, to debate. It is through dialogue that one discovers the convictions of others and one verifies the credibility of one's beliefs. Nothing is certain in advance: neither modernity nor authenticity. It is indeed this relationship between modernity and authenticity, unity and plurality, modern scientific efficacy and moral values that constructs a society.

Of course, it is difficult to connect meaning and logic, to tune them to each other. And yet we will keep trying. We do not wish to abandon the possibility of retaining an ethics, values, a deontology—because for us, freedom, meaning, and justice are connected. This also means that we believe strongly, as Jacques Derrida stresses, that plurality, the diversity of cultures and ways of life, deserves to be preserved and kept alive. We believe that either progress is absolute or there is none. Islam sees man as a totality and itself as a global and sovereign approach to this totality, while keeping itself, theoretically, from totalitarianism, a threat undermining all systems and dogmas.

Islam can contribute to the search for a balanced world, that is to say, a less dehumanized, more just, and more reasonable world. It is Islam that rejects the marginalization of religion under the pretext of progress. It also opposes the confusion of religion and politics, but does not lose sight of them, so that modern life is not transformed into a "nothing is religious," "nothing is political"—*everything is merchandise.* Islam is an atypical partner, unique and original, able to question certainties and able to contribute with its own stone to the building of a new universal that remains to be constructed.

Given the acceleration of the changes they are observing, it is up to Muslims to begin their internal revolution, or, at the very least, it is up to the inactive Muslim actors, who seem so unlike our forebears and ancestors, who made history and assumed their responsibilities as reasonable beings, natural beings, and religious beings, without confusing or opposing these different dimensions of life. Today, we cannot continue to be content with a decadence made worse by the promotion and the integration of technology and the exact sciences—that which is modernism but not authentic modernity. The authentic can lead to the global perspective and to the transcultural: this is the path we wish to follow. Through dialogue, we can perhaps reach a new universal. Alone, it is virtually impossible. In every case, the contemporary Muslim is beginning to question himself to reestablish, for and despite modernity, another sort of himself. We can no longer be content with repetitions of ourselves or imitations of the other.

I asked Derrida my question: given our knowledge that the world, if it is united, must also be plural and exist according to multiple modes, unlike civilizations that fear the right to difference, do you think that the civilization to come will be plural, or not?

Without hesitation, he replied, "I believe that plurality is the very essence of civilization. By plurality I mean that alterity, the principle of differences and the respect for alterity, are the principles of civilization. Therefore, I don't imagine a homogenous universal civilization; that would be the opposite of a civilization. We know today, for example, that a considerable number of languages are disappearing every day; I don't know the exact numbers, but I do know there are hundreds of languages and dialects that are disappearing, that a horrible linguistic hegemony is taking over the earth, and this is the opposite of civilization.

the absence of the divine, the exit of religion from life, a movement that the West has provoked, legitimized, and systematized. On the internal level, we are therefore confronted with various reactions to this: the politico–religious ideology that practices closure, under the pretext of responding to injustices; the violence of the powerful and the loss of meaning; the present regimes, which are tempted by the perpetuity of superficial democracy out of fear of instability or an insatiable appetite for power; and the "modernists," who are cut off from the masses and subjected to the temptation of frantic Westernization and wild liberalism under the pretext of emancipation.

On the external level, the will for domination and the egotism of certain Westerners, fed by technological supremacy, the imperatives of the market, and the retreat of interknowledge, make our burdens the following: the deformation of our values; the politics of double standards; the refusals and hesitations of the Northern shores to engage in a true dialogue, to imagine true negotiations; and finally, the notorious insufficiency of aid to the South. The world disorder, marked by the retreat of law, in fact concerns all peoples. The crisis is one of international law.

In dialogue with our neighbors, without resentment, and with the help of decisive allies like you, those who straddle the two shores can succeed, inspired by what that other Franco-Algerian, Jacques Berque, said: problems can be faced objectively. Con-

A civilization must be plural; it must ensure a respect for the multiplicity of languages, cultures, beliefs, ways of life. And it is in this plurality, in this alterity, that a chance—I won't speak of a solution—for the future is possible, namely, in multiplicity and plurality. Respect for this multiplicity and plurality is very difficult, because we must cultivate the idiom. What I call 'idiom' is the uniqueness of the language of the other, that is, the poetry of the other. There is no poetry and opening up without the idiom of the other. We must respect the idiom of each one of us, not only the so-called national idioms, but each person's idiom; this is his or her way of speaking, of being, and of signifying, while at the same time of communicating and translating. Consequently, we must translate. The task of translation is not incompatible with respect for the idiom—on the contrary. In principle, the idiom is untranslatable. But only that which is untranslatable calls for translation. For this plural civilization you are talking about, we must have the culture of unique idioms and of translatability, that is, universalization. We must keep them together; it's difficult, it's sometimes impossible, but it is the condition of this universal civilization you are talking about. The stakes have never been as high as they are in the world today; they are new stakes, which call for a new reflection on what 'universal' can mean and be. I appeal to the right to ask critical questions regarding not only the history of such and such a concept but also the history of the notion of criticism, the interrogative form of thought. Nothing should be sheltered from questioning, not even the classical figure of the universal and not even the traditional idea of criticism. It is clear that criticism, deconstruction, the work of thought can be said in the plural, a plurality of languages, cultures, and singularities."

With regard to my concerns, the essence of his philosophy had just been expressed: the work of thought starts from that elsewhere that is my own. This obvious fact, which so many malevolent types pretend to forget, seems essential to me. Both for non-Muslims and for Muslims, it is vital to remember that no one has the monopoly on the universal. It remains, today, for us to work together to rediscover a common universal. More than an hour and a half had gone by since the beginning of our session. I did not want to take advantage of his generosity. And so I decided to wrap things up by summarizing my point of view. I said, indeed, it is urgent to seek together a universal civilization that is sorely lacking. In spite of enormous progress, today there is no civilization. Abrahamic values, on the one hand, and democracy, on the other, are decreasingly influential. The threat of an increase in inequality and dehumanization is one of the traits of our era. Morality, ethics, the values of the spirit have left our lives. As we have stressed in self-critical terms, the citizen of the Southern shores

wants his neighbor on the Northern shore
the following: first, that politico-religious ε
is not Islam, even if the extremists speak in
It is usurpation. Especially since most of th
of this monstrosity are themselves Muslims.

In my country, Algeria, we know this and h
come it, thanks to the fact that, first, we have
fused Islamism and Islam and even less terro
Islam. And in the past, as you know, our ant
battle did not confuse the colonial State and
tianity. Second, authoritarian Arab regimes,
their occasional heterogeneous appearance and
the efforts made by some of them at reform,
societies whose greatest aspirations are the u
democratic values. We have to work toward
changes through internal negotiations, not t
interference. Nothing in our Islamic canon o
freedom as the foundation of existence. Third,
called modernist current, despite its opposition
rograde forces, does not represent the people wh
both modernity and authenticity and progress w
losing their roots.

It is a matter of undertaking these changes
out, in so doing, *crossing over to the West*, itself a n
in crisis, which has not assumed its responsibil
has not been able to teach us how to face up t
shrinking of meaning, which is a manifestatio
meaning, but also to the dissolution of the hori

sequently, people yearning for freedom, justice, and meaning, within the horizon of secularization and the democracy to come, have as a task to rethink a new relationship with the world and not fall into the trap of the battles that belong to the rearguard. Alone we cannot face up to this nor reason with desperate people if they remain repressed, dominated, or foreign to the life of the polis. Our future is linked, and you are our ally, our precious ally. The vicissitudes of modernity and the decline of our traditions cannot be corrected by unilateralism, but through common action, founded on a just understanding of the connection that must be formed between the specific and the universal. I looked at Derrida with gratitude and said to him, a thousand thanks for your patience and for everything you have said to us, taught us, and confided in us, for what you have told us, to us distant others—because we are fundamentally attached to a religious sense of the Mystery of life, of the world, and of that which is beyond the world—but who are so close, because we are also committed to secularity, to freedom, to being hospitable to the other recognized as other.

And I added, Professor Derrida, at the end of this meeting and in your very encouraging presence, allow me to say "the end" to our colloquium, a word of final closure, on behalf of all of us.

Showing emotion, he replied, "I thank you. And I want to repeat my gratitude for having been included in your work and in this discussion. I am very sensitive to the fact that we are 'among Algerians,' as you have said, I cherish that which is still Algerian in me, what is in me and keeps me Algerian."

Conclusion:
The Different Other
Is Indispensable to Our Lives

I offered these closing remarks while weighing and stressing each of my words, as if to mark the memorable character of our encounter, which, I believe, will not be forgotten, an encounter that was truly coming to an end. But the link that connects people committed to justice, meaning, and peace is infinite. And yet, for this inestimable link to be maintained, speech has to be addressed to the other, as Professor Jacques Derrida told us, and that depends on each of us, on our commitment to always prefer the Open. Our thanks to our great friend and compatriot Jacques Derrida, for his thoughtful, mediating words, his human voice, and his presence full of solidarity. Thanks to all who have participated in this colloquium, and to those who from yesterday to today have sympathized and sympathize with the Algerian people, throughout all its trials, its symbolic and physical *earthquakes,* including the struggle for liberation as a response to the rapacious domination of colonialism, the struggle against terrorist violence, that new cross-border monstrosity, and the earthquakes and other natural catastrophes.

The Algerian people, united, will not forget. More than ever, we cherish our friendship with the French people and the French nation in its diversity. This clearly means that the time is right for the serene memory of our history and for going beyond it: First, for us, people of the Southern shores, to forgive but not to forget—for the Northern shores, to put an end to the amnesia and recognize that there has been inadmissible violence; second, to adopt a method that favors dialogue, strategy, and the future; third, to understand that the multidimensional explanation is often the right path. This is at the heart of the path that leads to a renewal of our relations. We hope, we want to hope, for an exceptional relationship with France, based on reciprocal interests. We are two peoples at the forefront of relationships between worlds, shores, continents, civilizations. In the context of worldwide insecurity and injustice, faced with the difficulty of proposing a coherent project for society, with the crisis of meaning in the world, and after so many disappointments, dialogue and friendship between Algeria and France, between Maghreb and Europe, appear as avenues of hope: moreover, nobody can contest this dialogue and this friendship; one can say, in spite of differences, the heterogeneity and antagonisms, that they constitute the dialogue and the friendship between the East and the West.

We can resist new forms of colonialism, domination, depersonalization, which threaten all peoples without exception, if we know how to speak up rather than remain silent, to reflect and debate rather than choose hatred and implicit or declared violence. Dialogue, frank but peaceful and friendly discussion, is our choice, our destiny. In the face of the misdeeds of the past, of the colonizer who repressed an entire people through violence, the lives sacrificed during the war in Algeria showed that resistance was a legitimate language and the only imposed path necessary, the only possible alternative under these historical constraints. Thus the challenge of decolonization was issued, with its equal parts of light and shadow. Today, it is a matter of issuing a clearly laid out challenge of an open world order, of a coherent and just universal order, in dialogue, in negotiation, and in strict cooperation with our friends and other partners on the Northern shores. No country, no religion, no culture can, alone, open the horizon of a new relationship with the world. The right direction is the one that keeps alive the plurality of the world, of a just world. To work in this direction is certainly to attempt to forge a living awareness for future generations. If Algeria and France, which are so close geographically and historically, beyond the trials of the past and permanent altercations, don't provide a good example of rapprochement, exchange, and friendship, an example of how to build a common human space around the Mediterranean, a new Andalusia, that is so lacking, who will provide it?

Our colloquium, "Algeria-France: Tribute to the Great Figures of the Dialogue between Civilizations," is coming to a close, and we now have a task before us, one that is always incomplete: continuing to think, to analyze, and to discover how to live together, faithful to our roots, while respecting the other and in synch with the march of time. What we have just heard and said in the presence of one of the major thinkers of our time, Jacques Derrida, inspires us, invites us to act and to attempt to issue the challenges of our somber but surprising time. Our peoples are waiting to be inspired with reason, faith, and hope, not with fanaticism, irrationality, and despair.

This discussion hopes to be an invitation to integrate on every level, in school and university programs in our countries, the scientific study of religions, cultures, and civilizations, to learn how to deal with the multicultural, the critical spirit, and an opening up to the other. Our point of departure, the common denominator, is the reasonable reason mentioned more than forty-five times in the Koran. For us, beings of reason, this reasonable reason consists, in the first place, in keeping the final objective in sight, achieving the universal, the Open, living life humanely, in short, not turning our backs on the trial of the Absence-Presence of what is true; while for us, beings of faith, too, the meaning that is hidden is the meaning of the trial of existence. The Absent-Present is called the Divine, He whom nothing resembles, Who depends on no one, and is above everything. Next, reasonable reason implies facing together, reasonably and objectively, the multiple threats that lurk everywhere, inside and out, those of all the fundamentalisms and of the law of the strongest. Finally, that same reasonable reason demands that we be vigilant, so that justice and the law always take precedence in our actions, our relationships, and our projects. There is no peace, no future, without justice, without law, for problems are political. We must ally ourselves to work together to understand these concepts and to sketch peaceful and political solutions.

For us other Muslims, this also means revealing the virtualities, the possibilities, the invitations to freedom, responsibility, universal responsibility, contained in the Koran, inscribed in our history, and demanded by new generations. The democracy that is always still to come is founded on the right to criticize, as thinkers from Averroes to Rousseau, from Hegel to Derrida, have taught us, in a way that is relevant to our time. We need freedom, modernity, and progress without losing our souls. For our relationship to the Mystery is, for us others, children of Abraham, one of the foundations and essential dimensions of life. The connection between logic and meaning is at the heart of our concerns. Even if it is presented in a different way, the problem belongs to everyone, beginning with the West, the motor of modernity, with its prodigious advances founded on the unconditional exercise of Reason and its disturbing deviations, a sort of collusion between capitalism and atheism, but paradoxically also between these two and religious fundamentalism.

May the lives and works of historical figures such as Salahdin Ayubi and the emir Abdelkader, Saint Francis of Assisi and Raymond Lulle; of contemporary intellectuals from the two shores, committed to each other, faithful to the Open, such as Louis Massignon, Jacques Berque, and so many other intellectuals and thinkers, despite their differences, from Emmanuel Mounier to Blanchot, from Taha Hussein to Edward Said, from René Char to Mahmoud Derviche; may the thinking of philosophers such as Jacques Derrida; may the example of militant intellectuals such as André Mandouze; may the scholarly work of André Miquel; finally, may the voices of the just and the pious and those who anonymously support the weak, the poor, and the powerless continue to enlighten the spirit of our two peoples. May the

Conclusion

work of all of us, as Paul Ricoeur has written on the occasion of this colloquium, aim to *break down the walls of prejudice*, one's own and that of the other, in order to keep alive the idea of the human, the true, the beautiful, and the just that we all carry in us as our seed.

May the wheel of time not lock up on us, may the wheel of the world not grind up our differences, may the forgetting of that which is required of us be pushed aside—that the different other is indispensable to our lives is common sense: "If God had wanted it, he would have made you a single community, but he wanted, the Koran tells us, to test you through the gift of difference."

Afterword:
From the Southern Shores,
Adieu to Derrida

Madame Derrida, dear friends, ladies, gentlemen, I have come from Algiers, from El-Biar where I live, to share with you the huge sadness that envelopes us, we Algerians, and with us the peoples of the Southern shores. Jacques Derrida, our compatriot, was not only one of the greatest thinkers of our time—he was our ally. And he will remain the inestimable ally of all

This text, a farewell to Derrida following his death, was delivered on October 21, 2004, during the Rencontre mondiale organized by the Collège international de philosophie in Paris, under the heading "Farewell to Jacques Derrida." I thank Jean-Luc Nancy and Bruno Clément who kindly invited me. An Algerian had to be present to bear witness and mark his deep gratitude to "Jacques," our compatriot, our ally, our exemplary friend.

those who resist dehumanization and oppression. On the subject of the meaning of life, he left us a direction that is both different and close to the Abrahamic direction. So close, since hospitality, sacred hospitality, the welcoming of the other, the complete other, were for him also central to life. Different, because for him, even if nothing is given in advance and the risk of losing oneself remains entirely, the exercise of reason and thought must be carried out without conditions, as a chance for the advent of history. This friend, so dear, will not respond to our invitation, to which he had, in fact, given his enthusiastic agreement, in order to return to his native land for a pilgrimage, and to speak to us of our proximity and our difference, which are not in conflict.

He was a Jew. He was a philosopher. He taught us to think. He was a teacher. Today, more than ever, we must learn again from him, he who is henceforth and forever the present absent; we must learn how to face the political and religious problems of the world. In these somber times, we have such an acute need to rediscover a reasonable reason, in order to keep ourselves from a subjective approach, from myths and from denial, from what favors either an alienating herd instinct or a fatal closure. For us, Muslim intellectuals, his thinking opens up the path to a new encounter with the West. He is the one who testified with kindness and tenacity: "The world in which I speak is absolutely heterogeneous," he said.[1]

From our Mediterranean perspective, a tribute to this eminent thinker must begin by recalling his faithfulness to his roots on the Southern shores. In May 2003, on the occasion of the Year of Algeria in France, I had the honor of inviting him to participate in the closing session of a colloquium on the dialogue of civilizations, in a discussion on the relationship between Islam and the West. He quickly agreed to come.

Cruel fate, the very day of the encounter, he arrived directly from the hospital, shaken, with medical results in his hand. He told me, "For any other meeting I wouldn't have had the strength to participate." His arrival that day became the most beautiful sign of solidarity, the greatest gesture of friendship he could have offered: an overwhelming lesson of fraternity and courage. In addition, he told us of his compassion for Algeria, stricken three days earlier by a terrible earthquake, with such emotion that he seemed to forget the disturbing personal health news he had recently received! For more than an hour at the Institut du Monde Arabe, before an enthralled audience, so touched by his openness, we talked with this

1 From Jacques Derrida, "Fidélité à plus d'un—mériter d'hériter où la généalogie fait défaut," in "Rencontres de Rabat avec Jacques Derrida. Idiomes, nationalités, deconstructions" (speical issue), *Cahiers Intersignes* 13 (1998): 221–65.

Adieu to Derrida

vibrant teacher of humanity. He insisted on repeating, first of all, that he was Algerian, that he had left his native land only when he was nineteen years old. And to stress that, during the difficult days of the Second World War, it was above all the Muslims who had supported, comforted, and protected his family.

We talked about delicate subjects, with complete candor and the infinite respect for the other that he taught us in such an exemplary way. We addressed points of difference carefully and with attention: the question of the Mystery, of the relationship with the beyond and of the religious meaning of life and death. Without giving in on anything about anything, he asked himself, with an unbelievable strength, how to learn to live in a true, just, and beautiful way, if that is possible. For him, the point was to urge us to honor life and to go beyond an understanding of religion that mutates into "reactive antagonism and reaffirmative excess."[2]

The interruption of the life of one of the greatest thinkers of modernity is a painful trial, at the moment when we are witnessing the triumph of the law of the jungle, globalization's leveling to the lowest common denominator, and an increase in the terrorism of the weak and of the powerful as well as that of the right to die. We have lost a great ally in our

2 Jacques Derrida, *Foi et savoir*, Points Essais (Paris: Seuil, 2001), p. 10.

attempt to integrate modernity and to go beyond the risks that it engenders.

After the death ten years ago of Jacques Berque, that straddler of the two shores, as well as, four years ago, that of a lesser known figure whose contribution was decisive in the realm of thought, Gérard Granel, the traveling companion of he whom we are remembering today, the passing of Derrida makes us even more responsible for the legacy of dialogue and of critical thinking, a thinking that refuses to be abandoned to calculating logic and erupting hatred. At the passing of Gérard Granel, Derrida wrote to Jean Nancy: "The admiring friendship we share for the one who is no longer here . . . it is he . . . who irreplaceably will have rendered, renders, and will still render this sharing possible."[3] Isn't the same true of the one who today brings together the two shores of the Mediterranean, in sadness for his passing and in hope for his thinking? "Nothing essential," he asserted, "will be done if one doesn't allow oneself to be called forth by the other."[4] In his *Adieu* to Emmanuel Levinas, Derrida asked, "What happens then when a great thinker we have known alive, whom we have read, and reread, and also heard, is silenced, when we are still expecting to receive a response, as if it will

3 Jacques Derrida, *Granel: L'éclat, le combat, l'ouvert,* ed. Jean-Luc Nancy and Elisabeth Rigal (Paris: Belin, 2001), p. 139.

4 Derrida, "Fidélité à plus d'un—mériter d'hériter où la généalogie fait défaut."

Adieu to Derrida

help us not only to think otherwise, but even to read what we had believed to have already read under his signature, and who kept everything in reserve, and so much more than what we thought we had already understood?"[5] His response is a call for the tireless surprise of thinking.

Regarding Islam and the monstrous deviations that are occurring unjustly in its name, Derrida, unlike other intellectuals, stressed clearly, "Islam is not Islamism, never forget that."[6] He knew that one must not neglect the political motives that are expressed today in the form of religious fanaticism. He understood that the dissidence in the Muslim world and the culture of resistance in it were not merely reactionary and nihilistic but that they no doubt had causes that had to be taken into account, even if blind violence remains unjustifiable.

In writing one of his last works on democracy, hegemony, and world disorder, he called upon us: "The task consists in doing everything to help, first in the Islamic world, by allying ourselves with the forces that struggle not only for the secularization of the political . . . but also for an interpretation of the Koranic heritage that emphasizes from deep within potentialities, which are no doubt no more visible to the naked eye and by that name than they were in

5 Derrida, *Adieu à Levinas* (Paris: Galilée, 1997), pp. 21–22; English edition: *Adieu to Levinas* (Stanford, Calif.: Stanford University Press, 1999).

6 Derrida, *Foi et savoir,* p. 14.

the Old and the New Testaments." Adding that Islam was "the only religious culture that up to now would have resisted a European (Greco-Christian and globalization) process of secularization, thus of democratization, and therefore in the strict sense, of politicization."

This sentence forces us more than ever to look, through self-criticism, for the profound causes of our dissidence, by assessing that which is legitimate and that which is less so. We must thus demonstrate that, in our founding texts, the paradigm of freedom is central. Regarding the agreement between democracy with a given culture, Derrida wrote, "What isn't a given, is the institution of a problematic or of a task of this type . . . for every language and every non-Greek or non-European culture." But he added, "It presupposes . . . that there exists in Greek a single, stable and unique meaning of the democratic itself. But we are suspecting that this isn't true. . . . It is also a matter of a concept without a concept."[7]

This should inspire us to look together for the horizon of freedom and to create together the democracy to come—a philosophical, political, human project that Jacques Derrida opened up for us all. It is true that, on the one hand, in the Arab and Islamic regions, this reference to freedom experiences disturbing and unacceptable internal contradictions and

7 Jacques Derrida, *Voyous* (Paris: Galilée, 2003), pp. 54–57.

turbulence and that, on the other, there exists, on the part of strangers, a lack of understanding and a number of prejudices that distort the discussion about the distinctiveness of the Muslim, who is attached both to Revelation and responsibility.

In the last telephone conversation I had with Derrida in the summer of 2004, I spoke to him of my essay on the relationship to the other in Islam, *L'Islam: Tolérant ou intolérant?*, and of my intention to focus on the open, spiritual, and religious dimension of Islam, in contrast to the instrumentalization of religion to political ends; he essentially told me the question of the relationship to the other, just like the question of freedom, which is intimately linked to it, are major themes to explain and to clarify, but not the only ones that constitute the foundation of existence.

He taught us that critical and objective thinking, "deconstruction," if there is any, speaks more than one language and more than one culture, since it aims at existence. For the philosopher, it is obvious that each moment of this experience is linked to figures of singularity. It was not just because Algeria was his native land that Derrida loved it; it was also because of its deep acknowledgment of the singularity of the other. We can say this with gratitude: his thinking has contributed to advancing our attempt at a reflection on the destiny of Islam, that religion that is concerned, more than others, with the break between logic and meaning, with the break between the temporal and the spiritual, that break defined by Berque as "a cave dug in the existence of contemporary man."[8]

Jacques Derrida lived, with generosity and constancy, a faithfulness to more than one identity, as a Frenchman, as an Algerian, as a Jew, as a citizen of the world, concerned with truth and rapprochement. The fact that *Specters of Marx*, for example, was translated into Arabic by a Lebanese woman touched him. A concern haunted him: we never worry enough about the rest of the world, never enough! How can we forget Jacques Derrida!

He was of the two shores, he came from the edge of the world. In concert with his friend Granel,[9] he adopted the belief that "the peoples of mortality are not two, but three: Greek, Jewish, Arab." Algeria and the entire Arab world are going to greatly miss the company of this other who was so close, of this friend, companion, in Arabic *uns*. Through his way of questioning, he brought to life our communion, the *mu'àchara*, with the West, and prevented the despair of the other.

8 Jacques Berque, *L'Islam au temps du monde* (Arles: Actes Sud, 2002), p. 239.

9 Gérard Granel, "Sibboleth ou de la lettre," *Revue philosophique* (Paris) 115, no. 2 (1990): 185–206.

Biography:
Derrida and the Southern Shores

1930: Birth of Jacques Derrida, July 15, in El-Biar
(Algiers, Algeria).

1934: His family leaves the rue Saint-Augustin in
Algiers to settle in El-Biar.

1935–1941: Early education in El-Biar. In 1941, laws of
the Pétain regime in the school: Article 2 of the Status
of Jews of October 3, 1940, excluded them from education and from justice.

1941: Jacques Derrida enters into *sixième* at the Lycée
Ben Aknoun, on the outskirts of El-Biar.

1942: Derrida must leave the lycée. The anti-Semitism
(anti-Arab and anti-Jewish) of the colonists runs

rampant. Derrida enrolls, until the spring of 1943, in the Lycée Émile-Maupas, the name of the street in which, behind the cathedral of Algiers, the Jewish teachers prohibited from teaching in government schools had temporarily set up a school. In these years, the question of the unique nature of Jacques Derrida's adherence to Judaism begins to be raised: his wounded, painful sensitivity to anti-Semitism as well as to all racism, the response of someone "hypersensitive" to xenophobia, but also impatience with gregarious identification, before the militantism of adherence.

1943–1947: Return to the Lycée Ben Aknoun, a disorganized, unruly, and athletic academic environment. Dreams of becoming a professional soccer player. Pursues his studies. At the same time, develops a taste for intellectual issues; has trouble adapting, retreats, keeps "personal journal," read intensely (Rousseau, Gide, Nietzsche, Camus).

1947–1948: Philosophy class at the Lycée Gauthier in Algiers.

1948–1949: Begins to focus more seriously on philosophy. Reads Kierkegaard and Heidegger.

1949–1950: First trip to the "mainland," to Marseille. Studies at Louis-le-Grand. Recalls his intense reading of Simone Weil, the "existentialists," essays described as "Plotinian" by Étienne Borne, and theories of the time (Sartre, Marcel, Merleau-Ponty).

1950–1951: Still second-year boarding student at Louis-le-Grand. Difficult living conditions. Poor health. Return to El-Biar for three months.

1951–1952: Third year of studies at Louis-le-Grand, where he meets some of those who essentially remained his friends, many of whom he later met again at the École normale supérieure, which he entered at the end of the year (among others, Lucien Bianco, Pierre Bourdieu, Michel Deguy, Gérard Granel, Pierre Nora, Louis Marin, Michel Serres).

1952–1953: École normale supérieure. Immediately gets to know Althusser (who was also born in Algiers), and they become friends; some twenty years later, they become colleagues. Beginning of a new degree course.

1956–1957: Passes his *agrégation* for teaching; receives a scholarship as "special auditor" at Harvard University in Cambridge. Reads Joyce. In June 1957, in Boston, marries Marguerite Aucouturier (they have two sons, Pierre, born in 1963, and Jean, born in 1967).

1957–1959: Military service during the Algerian War. An intellectual concerned with coexistence, peace, and justice, he asks to be assigned to a post as teacher. He succeeds and is placed in an elementary school for children of soldiers (Koléa, near Algiers). For more than two years, he is a second-class civilian soldier, teaching French and English to young Algerians or French students from Algeria. Lives with Marguerite and his friends the Biancos in a villa in Koléa, teaching in a private school, and translates press releases. Often meets with Bourdieu in Algiers. Derrida always condemned French colonial policy in Algeria but hoped, up to the last moment in 1962, that a form of independence would be invented that would make it possible to cohabitate with the French from Algeria. He even tried to convince his parents not to leave Algeria in 1962. Derrida often spoke of his "*nostalgérie*."

1962: His family leaves Algeria. Between 1962 and 1964, he teaches at the Sorbonne as an assistant with Bachelard and Ricoeur, and then is accepted into the Centre national de la recherche scientifique and the École normale supérieure.

1966: Participates in a colloquium in Baltimore (Johns Hopkins University) that was later to become famous—and that marked the beginning of an intensification in the arrival of certain French philosophers or theoreticians in the United States. Derrida meets Paul de Man and Jacques Lacan and sees Hyppolite, Vernant, and Goldman there.

1971: First return to Algeria since 1962. Sees the "garden" and Tipaza again. Lectures and teaches at the University of Algiers. The Algerians are happy to have him back, and for him, as well, it is a humanly "historic" moment, a return to his roots.

1979: He takes the initiative, with other intellectuals, to convene the Estates General of Philosophy. And he always remains attached to his "elsewhere," Africa. First trip to black Africa for the Cotonou meeting.

1980: Defense of his thesis at the Sorbonne. Opening of the French Congrès de philosophie in Strasbourg. Later that year, he is the focus of a ten-day conference, organized by Philippe Lacoue-Labarthe and Jean-Luc Nancy, and, no doubt, with Gérard Granel, among other French philosophers closest to Derrida in thinking and friendship, who also supported a thinking that welcomes and respects the other.

1981: In this fertile relationship with the rest of the world, along with Jean-Pierre Vernant and a few friends, he establishes the Jan Hus Association (aiding dissident or persecuted Czech intellectuals), of which he was vice president.

1982: The vast, the international, the universal are increasingly his realms of interest. Asked by J.-P. Chevènement, another political friend from the South, to coordinate a mission (made up of François Châtelet, Jean-Pierre Faye, and Dominique Lecourt), he reflects on the principle of creating an international college of philosophy and consults his friend Emmanuel Levinas. First trips to Japan and Mexico. First of a series of trips to Morocco at the invitation of his friend Abdelkebir Khatibi. Regular seminar at San

Sebastian. Named A. D. White Professor at Large at
Cornell University.

1983: Founding of the International College of
Philosophy, of which Derrida is the first elected
director. He participates in the organization of the
exposition "Art against Apartheid" and in the initiatives aimed at creating the Cultural Foundation
against Apartheid (of which Derrida is a member of
the governing board) and in the committee of writers
for Nelson Mandela. Accepted at the École des hautes
études en sciences sociales (field of study: philosophical institutions).

1984: Trip to Japan. Frankfurt: lecture at the Habermas
seminar and opening lecture of the Joyce colloquium
in Frankfurt (Ulysse Gramophone).

1985: First trip to Latin America (Montevideo, Buenos
Aires). Meets Jorge Luis Borges.

1988: Third trip to Jerusalem. Meets with Palestinian
intellectuals and visits the occupied territories. Writes
"Interpretations at War" with Moshe Ron.[1]

1989: Opening speech at the colloquium organized
by the Cardozo School of Law in New York, on

1 Jacques Derrida and Moshe Ron, "Interpretations at War: Kant, the Jew, the
German," in "Institutions of Interpretation," special issue, *New Literary History*
22, no. 1 (Winter 1991): 39–95.

Biography

deconstruction and the possibility of justice. This colloquium marks an important step in the rapid development of his "deconstructive" research in philosophy and in theory of the law (critical legal studies) in the United States. Copresident, with Jacques Bouveresse, of the Commission de réflexion pour l'épistémologie et la philosophie.

1991: Invitation from the Algerian ministry of higher education, which I directed, to Derrida and Granel, to participate in Algiers in a colloquium on "the relationship between the West and Islam." Despite the agreement in principle by the two philosophers, the colloquium could not take place due to the first Gulf War.

1996: Publication of *Le Monolinguisme de l'autre*, in which he returns to his relationship with languages, and through that also to Maghrebin culture. Meeting in Rabat on the theme "languages, nationalities, deconstructions," with Derrida and Maghrebin, Arab and French scholars, where analyses are sketched on the deconstruction at work concerning the Southern shores.

2003: Meeting at the Institut du monde arabe. Colloquium on "The Future of Civilizations," on the occasion of the "Year of Algeria in France"; Derrida participates in the closing session, a discussion on the East/West relationship, the relationship between the two shores, in the face of current challenges. Derrida

Derrida and the Southern Shores

accepts the invitation to again come to Algeria in the autumn of 2004. Fate decides otherwise. This same year, 2003, he publishes *Voyous,* his decisive book on political philosophy.

2004: October 21, 2004, in Paris, rue Descartes, world day of affectionate tribute, a farewell, "of sorrow and of speech" to Jacques Derrida, organized by the International College of Philosophy. At the invitation of Bruno Clément, president of the College, and of Jean-Luc Nancy, I felt I was representing all of Algeria as a testimony to our connection and to our gratitude to the Franco-Algerian philosopher.

2006: International colloquium in Algiers on November 25 and 26 in memory of Derrida. Two years after the passing of Jacques Derrida, Algeria, the country of his birth, pays tribute to him. To remember and to recall the modern, living, and open thinking of Jacques Derrida, who so defended the law, justice, and democracy, *always to come,* is to continue his universal battle of ideas, subversive in the noble sense of the term.